Breakfast Sausage Bake
(Quiches)

Ham casserole
Ham + Potato casserole) pg. 96

Baked catfish pg. 98

So Fat, Low Fat, No Fat

Betty Rohde

A FIRESIDE BOOK
Published by Simon & Schuster
New York   London   Toronto   Sydney   Tokyo   Singapore

This book is dedicated to my husband Bob Rohde, without whose love, understanding, and concern I could not have written it. I am yet to figure out if he is glad or sad that it is finished, because every night he has eaten something new and different, maybe not yet worked out completely but he ate it anyway and helped with his critiquing of the results. Not always good, I must add. The Persimmon Pudding must have been the worst! Recipe NOT included.

■ ■ ■ ■ ■ ■ ■ ■ ■ ■ ■ ■ ■ ■ ■ ■ ■ ■ ■ ■

 FIRESIDE

Rockefeller Center
1230 Avenue of the Americas
New York, New York 10020

Copyright © 1993 by Betty Rohde

Published by arrangement with the author

First Fireside Edition 1995

FIRESIDE and colophon are registered trademarks of Simon & Schuster Inc.

Designed by Bonni Leon
Manufactured in the United States of America

20   19   18   17   16   15

Library of Congress Cataloging-in-Publication Data

Rohde, Betty
    So fat, low fat, no fat/Betty Rohde. — 1st Fireside ed.
      p.   cm.
    "A Fireside book."
    Previously published as: Recipes. Waseca, MN : Walter's Cookbooks, 1993.
    Includes index.
    1. Low-fat diet—Recipes.   I. Title.
RM237.7R628   1995
641.5'638   dc20   94-38741
                                                              CIP

ISBN: 0-671-89813-2

CONTENTS

Mushroom Dill chix w/ Stove Top   pg. 66

■ ■ ■ ■ ■ ■ ■ ■ ■ ■ ■ ■ ■ ■ ■ ■ ■ ■

Introduction

HOW I LOST 40 POUNDS
IN 6 MONTHS
WITHOUT EVER BEING HUNGRY,
WAS STABLE FOR 3 MONTHS,
LOST 20 MORE POUNDS
IN THE NEXT 3 MONTHS,
LOWERED MY CHOLESTEROL
FROM 274 TO 210
IN THE FIRST 6 MONTHS, AND
LOWERED MY TRIGLYCERIDES
FROM 678 TO 240
IN THE FIRST 6 MONTHS

I had been having health problems for some time and was feeling very depressed. I finally made a visit to the doctor for a checkup, and what I found was not at all a pretty picture. My doctor told me, "Lady, you're a walking time bomb." I was sitting on my porch when I got the phone call from him advising me of my terribly high counts. After our conversation, I sat there looking at the spring that was coming alive. We live in the country in a big Victorian-style house that is just a few years old, with all the beauty surrounding us that many dream of in fairytale books.

My family is close, my town is clean, my church is alive and growing, my friends are fun, my husband is supportive—what more could a person ask? I believe that was the moment I decided that I and I alone had to do something to improve my health and just maybe I better listen to Mr. Doctor Man.

I knew that I had to completely change my life and the way I ate, the way I shopped, the way I cooked, even the way I thought. That may just have been the real challenge.

I made dinner that night, cooking the old standby for dieters: broiled chicken breast and steamed vegetables. I sat there eating that tasteless meal knowing that this would be it for some time. I made up my mind that I was going to do something about my eating and health, but that I also was going to have something that was fit to eat, that tasted as good as the things I was used to eating and was at the same time helping me to improve my health.

This book will show you how I changed, rearranged, and developed my techniques. The book came to be after the first six months and I had lost forty pounds, was never hungry, never felt deprived or that I was missing anything except the fat that I had lost and I was glad to be missing that. Think of this: I was a tight size 16, now I am a 10. This was the most fun: all new clothes, plus the fun of people not knowing me. I stood and talked to a former neighbor at a Christmas party that I had not seen for over a year and she did not know me. Of course I did get a new hairdo, contacts, the works. Now, ladies, this is fun—try it. It was the easiest thing I have ever done to lose weight, and believe me I have been on *all* the diets, have lost more than I weigh three times over. The nicest thing is that I have *never* even gained one pound back. Taking it off this way keeps it off, unlike so many fad diets, where the weight comes back as soon as you get it off. You get used to eating and cooking fat-free and the weight stays off.

I had full balanced meals, entertained, ate out, baked and snacked along with our daily routines, with only a little effort and thought as to how and what I was doing with my food. It has become an effortless way of life. I don't even look for the oil in the kitchen but I do still use my skillet, as explained in this book.

I have learned moderation and balance rather than deprivation and starvation. I eat as much as I want of anything that I want as long as it is fat-free. I have never limited my portion sizes. I would have lost faster probably if I had, but well enough should be left alone. I wish you could have seen my doctor's face when he saw me—I had lost the first forty pounds without seeing him. He is so proud of me, he now uses my book and recommends it to his patients. I have learned and am enjoying the skills, techniques, and resources for healthy eating.

I love food, preparing it, experimenting with it, tasting it, talking about it, and entertaining with it. The meals I serve certainly do not skimp on the flavor or the portions. We entertain a lot, and after the first six months my friends kept saying I should write these recipes down, put some of these ideas in a book—it was working for me and why should it not be working for other people? I am grateful for the encouragement and support that led to the publication of *So Fat Low Fat No Fat*. I have met so many new friends, which is as much of an asset as anyone could ask. The moral is: Ladies, it is never too late; all you have to do is to make up your mind. I have started a complete new life and career. You never know what lies around the corner.

I never dreamed this would happen to me when I wrote my book. I made my first order for just two hundred books. It was such a hit because it is good basic down-home easy recipes. Ladies, take heed! It is *never* too late. Start *today*!!!

I started by going to the grocery store the first day for about a two-hour visit. You have to read the labels. I read everything in that store, I thought. Soon it became a challenge to see what I could find fat-free, then it became a game. It is fun. Every day since I started it seems there has been some new product on the market. When this first started for me there was very little out, but for you starting now this is going to be really easy: the market is full of fat-free products.

One day I explored in the candy counter. I read every label on that counter and came home with a basketful of candy. I was so happy, because I am a sugar freak! I know it is bad for me and if you can you should try to limit your sugar intake. This is what I told my doctor when he said to me that if I had limited my sugar and exercised I would have lost more, faster. My reply was this: "If I had cut out the fat, cut out the sugar, limited my portion sizes, and exercised myself weak, I would have lasted about two weeks." He said I was probably right, and whatever I was doing or not doing, to keep it up.

If you are wondering just what *would* I eat, here are some ideas:

Breakfast is easy. You can have an English muffin (1 gram of fat) with jelly (jelly has no fat grams). Leave *off* the butter; you'll never miss the butter after a couple of weeks. (There is a fat-free margarine on the market now; you be the judge.) I use fat-free cream cheese on the toasted muffin or bagel, or on toast—fat-free bread of course. There are so many cereals out now that are fat-free. Try them with skim milk (read your labels; just because they say "skim" does not mean they are fat-free), juice, and if you are an egg person, try scrambling some egg substitute—after about the second time you won't know the difference. We even make sandwiches in the evening with egg substitute. This is a pretty healthy breakfast, and if you had eaten everything I named you would have only had 1 gram of fat.

Lunch is just as easy—use your thinker! Brown-bag it. We do. It is economical, convenient, and healthy. And it leaves you more time to do something else, like shopping or visiting. Example: bread (fat-free), mayonnaise (fat-free), lettuce, tomato, pickle, mustard (all fat-free). Use 98 percent fat-free turkey, ham, or whatever lunch meat you like that is low in fat and you have a wonderful sandwich. You may prefer to take soup (there are plenty of fat-free soups), and a salad with fat-free dressing. You can even have fat-free cookies, cake, or candy. So far today you have had about 4 grams of fat. You're doing good!

Dinner: If you go out, choose your restaurants carefully. Beware of the places that are greasy: *keep away.* You are usually better off with a buffet-style dinner, but ordering from the menu is also easy. Order fish baked (I don't like fish so I choose something else), broiled, or poached; chicken baked, broiled, or stir-fried. Order steamed vegetables, which is what most restaurants do anyway because of the preparation time—just ask them to leave off the butter. Take your own dressing for the salad (and you should try it on a baked potato—pretty good). Be sure you always ask at every restaurant, "Do you have fat-free?" More and more establishments are starting to have low-fat and/or no-fat entries. The more we ask, the more we will be able to get them to carry. Most cafeterias will give you a vegetable plate, with three vegetables. I order mashed potatoes with no gravy or a baked potato, and a couple of veggies that look lower in seasoning—usually the broccoli without the cheese sauce and a bean of some sort.

Dessert: Forget it until you get home: this will take care of the late-night snackies anyway. I keep fat-free yogurt or ice cream on hand and fat-free cookies—that is, if I haven't had time to bake or don't have any cake around. You can stop at some ice cream establishments and get fat-free cones if you are making a night of it.

So far this one day you have had about 10 grams of fat at the most. This is what I kept my intake to, but then my doctor told me I would lose weight on 30 to 50 grams a day. I was so mad at me that I had cut to 10—but it was so easy I was surprised. I am sure that I sometimes ate more than 10 grams because I have to rely on the manufacturers' labels entirely.

I have given you an example of a day away from home. Now you can choose your meals from this book and have just as low a count. Plus sometimes you can have leftovers for your lunch next day. Everything that you could possibly need is included: entertaining, Mexican, Italian, Greek, American, and most of all, good basic down-home old-fashioned cooking without having to go to a specialty shop for your ingredients. I use everyday staples; you won't have to buy a $3.00 bottle of special seasoning for one dish and have it for the rest of your life. How many of you have that jar of weird seasoning that you have had ever since you can remember and it is starting to crystallize around the lid? I think that we all have one of those souvenirs. I live in Gore, America, with one *small* grocery store here and if I can find the ingredients here you can find them *any*where.

My recipes will help you to continue with or to start your fat-free or low-fat eating habits as well as trim your figure. I wish I had kept a log of the number of people who have come to me and said, "I have been just cooking strictly out of this book and I have lost X number of pounds in the last so many weeks or months." I have many women come to me and say, "My husband just had open heart surgery and we are now on the fat-free and he is really loving the recipes I make from your book because they taste just like normal."

After you have been on the fat-free for a couple of weeks and get used to not eating the fat, when you do eat something that is fat, your mouth will feel greasy. You will say, "*Yuck!*" One bite is all that it takes. I have numerous people ask me, "Don't you ever binge, or pig out on something that you are not supposed to eat?" My feeling is that it is not worth it. It sometimes makes me sick if I do eat even a small amount of grease, and that makes me happy, as it is like alcohol. I am happy to have the "fat habit" broken. I want it to make me sick so that I will know if I do eat it what will happen, and it is easier to just say, "No, thank you."

Include lots of fresh fruit in your daily eating. I am one of the unlucky ones who do not like fruit, so this is another hardship when trying to diet. Three things that I hate: fruit, fish, exercise. This is why I feel that I have found the secret, I have lost all this weight without those three demons. I have cut out red meat; it is said to have the largest percentage of fat of anything in our diets. I will have a filet on special occasions, but when I do, I have a baked potato and salad and skip the bread. I take my own salad dressing, don't eat the bacon around the steak, and I am OK. Just don't do it every day. Moderation. I must admit I have not had a hamburger in two years, nor a french fry. You know what? I don't even miss them. In the summer we make chicken patties, grill them on the barbie, and use our burger just as if it were beef. They are pretty good, and look at all the grams I saved!

"Eating at her house is not what it used to be, but it's not bad," said my brother.

I can guarantee you will lose weight if you do exactly as I tell you: Eat one page a day out of this book with 8 ounces of water and you will lose weight. Ha! Now try the recipes and you *will* lose weight.

For more information or if you have questions or comments, please write to:

Betty Rohde
P.O. Box 37
Gore, OK 74435

NOTE

The number of grams of fat listed per recipe is for the entire dish unless indicated otherwise.

Tidbits

Helpful Hints

1. Read your labels for the amount of fat. Items alike and side by side will have differing amounts of fat in each product.
2. Just because the label says "skim milk" does not mean that it is free of fat. Choose the one that lists zero fat on the label.
3. "Light" or "Lite" or "Low-fat" labels—skip them. Read the amount of fat contained and go for the fat-free labels, listing 0 fat grams. The markets are carrying more and more of these each day.
4. Any beef cut that ends in the word "loin," such as "tenderloin," is one of the leaner cuts.
5. Sugar can be reduced by at least one third in baked goods without affecting the final product.
6. Make mashed potatoes with skim milk and Butter Buds. Also, use some of the water they were cooked in to whip them fluffy. Or you can make mashed potatoes with skim milk or low-fat buttermilk instead of milk and butter. Very good. The buttermilk will give them a butter flavor.
7. Experiment with nonfat yogurt and no-fat sour cream. In hot dishes, add 1 teaspoon of cornstarch for every cup of yogurt to keep it from separating on heat.
8. Use ground turkey instead of ground beef. Substitute turkey or chicken cutlets for veal. Watch your turkey—buy only fresh-ground, or have your butcher grind it for you. The kind that comes in rolls like pork sausage has too much fat. Read the labels!
9. Try whipping very cold or partially frozen evaporated skim milk in place of heavy cream. (Chill the beaters and bowl in the freezer first.)
10. Use mashed potatoes instead of cream to thicken sauces, soups, and gravies.
11. Refrigerate soups and stews until fat congeals on top to make fat removal easier. If time does not permit, use a paper towel to soak up the surface fat or use a defatting pitcher. They pour from the bottom and leave the fat in the container.
12. Chips: For low-fat chips, cut corn or flour tortillas or pita bread into wedges. Bake until crisp. Use instead of potato chips.

13. You can substitute applesauce for oil in any pie, cake mix, or brownies.
14. Use the equivalent amount of egg substitute or egg whites for the number of eggs called for in baking.
15. Sauté: To sauté anything—veggies, et cetera—just cook it quickly in $1/4$ cup or so of water until transparent or tender. It works just as well as oil, and without the fat.
16. To cook beans or greens the Southern way, or to make stew or soups, cook whatever meat is desired for flavor—ham, beef, chicken, etc. Defat the liquid with defatting pitcher or refrigerate overnight and take congealed fat off the top. Then cook the beans or whatever in this liquid for the desired flavor without the fat.
17. Tomato juice will stimulate the kidneys and prompt them to filter out quantities of fatty deposits from the bloodstream, according to *Global Mini Mag*.
18. Because fat enhances the flavor of food, spices should be increased by 50 percent when developing low-fat versions of traditional cookies.
19. Sour cream substitute: 1 cup of no-fat cottage cheese mixed with 1 tablespoon of lemon juice and 2 tablespoons of skim milk. Blend well. There's also a recipe for Mock Sour Cream on page 213.
20. Hold the frosting: Dust your cake with cocoa and cinnamon or confectioners' sugar.
21. Instead of using sour cream in your recipe, substitute an equal amount of (skim) buttermilk.
22. Instead of potato chips, eat Crispix cereal. No fat, and they are good with your sandwich.
23. When making your sandwich, if you watch what you're doing, you can have a very low-fat sandwich. Fat-free bread, mayonnaise, cheese, lettuce, pickle, and meat that is 98 percent fat-free. What more do you need?
24. Some candy is fat-free; read the label. Candy corn, dinner mints, marshmallow peanuts, hard candies, etc.
25. When you brown ground turkey, sausage, or beef, put the browned meat in a colander and rinse with hot water. Shake off any excess water. This will help to wash away just a few more grams of fat.
26. Dark-meat chicken has 50 percent more fat than white meat. I use only boneless, skinless white meat. You say it costs more, figure this: you throw away the skin, the bones, and aren't going to eat the dark

meat. How much did that cost? You might as well just pay for what you are going to eat and feel better about saving fat grams and time in preparing.

27. Broccoli has beta carotene as well as sulforophane, a powerful natural chemical that helps protect against cancer. I eat broccoli at least once a week. No fat—no heart disease—no cancer—no kidding.

28. Use more rice, baked potatoes, cereals (fat-free), vegetables, and pasta in your diet. Not only do these foods contain virtually no fat but they are more efficient and readily available fuel for your muscles and they help sustain energy levels over long periods of time.

29. Count your fat grams and you don't have to worry about the calories. I never counted anything except the fat grams—my doctor says that is all you need to worry about. But here is the formula just in case you want to do the math trick (which I never did; it is too hard, keeps you confused. All I did was say 1 gram plus 2 grams plus 3 grams, etc. That is the simple way and it *works*!!!

Multiply the number of grams of fat by 9 and divide by the total number of calories in the dish. For example, if a frozen dinner provides 300 calories and contains 12 grams of fat, the percentage of fat calories is 12 x 9 divided by 300 = .36 or 36 percent.

Fat contains 9 calories per gram—more than twice as many as carbohydrate or protein, each of which contain 4 calories per gram. Foods rated at 20 percent fat or less are recommended for regular consumption. Foods rated at 20 percent to 40 percent are to be used in moderation provided that most of your diet comes from lower-fat foods. (The exception is fish, which protects your cardiovascular system.)

Many foods that we think are high in protein are actually higher in fat. Frankfurters, sausage, most lunch meats, and hamburger, for example, are high-protein foods that are 50 percent to 80 percent fat in terms of percentage of calories.

KEYS TO LIFELONG WEIGHT CONTROL

1. *Avoid fat foods.*
2. *Eat lots of whole grains, whole fruits, beans, and most vegetables,* which are good sources of high-fiber foods. Dietary fiber has a bulking effect that can aid in appetite control.
3. *Exercise.* The calories burned during exercise boost your metabolic rate and increase your body's capacity to burn fat.

"The single most influential dietary change one can make to lower the risk of these diseases is to reduce intake of foods high in fat and to increase the intake of foods high in complex carbohydrates and fiber."
— The Surgeon General's Report on Nutrition and Health (1988)

"It is calculated that, if intake of dietary fat were reduced from the present 40 percent of total calorie intake to 25 percent, about 9,000 lives would be saved annually."
— National Cancer Institute, Annual Review of Public Health

"Eating less fat can reduce the risk of colon, prostate, and breast cancer."
— National Research Council, "Diet and Health" (1989)

ABCs of Cutting Fat

ALTERNATIVES: Save fat and calories by switching from regularly used cheese, sour cream, etc., to fat-free.

BALANCE: Balance your food choices. If you eat a meal that is higher in fat than you know you should be eating, make the next one low-fat or no-fat. If you have something moderately high in fat, balance it with steamed veggies or items with no fat.

CELEBRATIONS: Don't fall victim; choose low-fat or no-fat dips, tortilla chips, angel food cakes. There are so many chips, etc., on the market you can really just about have everything you would normally but *fat-free.*

DRESSINGS: Fat-free bottled dressings taste just as good as their heavy-weight brothers and sisters. Carry them with you in your purse—they can be used on everything. (Well, maybe not ice cream.)

EXERCISE: Exercise is as important as a good diet (I hate it!!). Walking will do just as well, but walk briskly for 30 minutes three or four times a week.

FAST FOOD: Forget it, folks. If you find yourself in this position, choose the salad bar with caution. Remember to take your own dressing.

GUILT: Don't be too hard on yourself. Food is meant to be enjoyed—just be careful how good a time you have. And be more careful how you prepare it. If you go overboard one day, ease up the next.

HALF: If you can't resist something illegal, halve it or share with a skinny friend. (We all have *one* of those!)

ICE: Try fruit ices, sorbet, or sherbets.

JUNK FOOD: Keep healthy nibbles on hand. Try low-fat and no-fat pretzels, baked tortilla chips, etc.

KICK THE HABIT: Once you kick the fry habit, you've got it made. A few minutes more to prepare, a lot less fat grams to wear.

LABELS: Read *all* labels before buying. The 0 fat labels are what you're looking for. If it says "zero fat grams" it is in my basket, I don't care what it is! My husband just warned me, "Stay out of the dog food section. Please."

MIDMORNING: If a midmorning snack is a part of your day, pass up the pastry; go for fruit or an English muffin.

NONSTICK: These pans greatly reduce and/or eliminate fat when cooking.

OIL: Oil gets 100 percent of its calories from fat. Use with caution and care, and choose canola, olive, and/or safflower. Better yet—*omit!*

PORTIONS: Reduce your portion size to help reduce your own size.

QUESTIONS: Ask lots—about "Do you have fat-free?" at restaurants and/or grocery stores or "Will you get fat-free?" The more we ask, the more they will carry or have at restaurants.

REFRIGERATE: Broths, stews, and soups, to collect any sneaky fats that are hiding from you.

STEAM: Change to steamed vegetables. Steaming saves vitamins and nutrients and uses no fat.

TRIM: Remove all visible fat and skin before cooking meats.

UNADORNED: You'll really be amazed at how much flavor you're missing by drowning vegetables in butter, sauces, and dressings. Let the real flavor shine through. Eat them steamed or raw.

VARIETY: Don't get into a slump and think you can only eat special or limited foods on a healthy diet. Shop wise and eat many varieties.

WHITES: Substitute 2 egg whites for 1 egg in any recipe. It works, and you'll never know the difference but your heart will.

XXXX SUGAR: Confectioners' or powdered sugar is labeled XXXX sugar. Keep it on hand to sprinkle on cakes or to make a little light sauce for angel food cakes or fresh fruit. (Also means kisses when you send hugs 0000.)

YOGURT: Frozen fat-free now comes in many flavors. It's great. Look for fat-free yogurt and ice cream; some is fat-free and sugar-free, and is delicious to say the least.

ZIPPER BAGS: Cut up veggies to have on hand and store in zipper bags. How did we live without them?

Tips for Working Women

THINGS TO KEEP ON HAND FOR QUICK, EASY COOKING IN MINUTES

Breaded chicken tenders
Oriental frozen stir-fry vegetables
Frozen chopped onions
Frozen chopped green peppers
Fat-free chicken broth
Canned tomatoes—stewed
Dried macaroni
Frozen breaded fish fillets
Frozen chicken patties for burgers

SNACKS

Keep snacks in your purse, briefcase, gym bag, car, etc. Eating a fat-free snack several times a day is better than one burger or candy bar. I eat as much and as often as I want as long as it is fat-free.

Bagels
Breadsticks
Dry cereal—fat-free
Fig bars—fat-free
Granola bars—fat-free
Popcorn cakes
Rice cakes
Pretzels—fat-free
Raw vegetables
Vegetable juice
Fresh fruit

Dried fruit
Frozen juice bars
Fat-free ice cream
Fat-free frozen yogurt
Nonfat yogurt
String cheese—fat-free
Skim chocolate milk
Lunch meat (95% to 98% fat-free)
Water-packed tuna
Turkey breast meat

Appetizers

BAKED SOUTHERN DIP

This is pretty to serve for the holidays.

1 round loaf pumpernickel bread, unsliced
1 (8-ounce) package fat-free cream cheese, softened
½ cup fat-free sour cream
1 teaspoon cornstarch
¼ cup salsa (hot)
1½ cups shredded fat-free Cheddar cheese
Fresh vegetable sticks

SERVES 6
TO 8

LESS THAN 1
GRAM FAT

Prep :15
Cook 1:00
Stand :00
Total 1:15

Preheat the oven to 350 degrees. Cut a ¼-inch slice off the top of the bread. Set aside.

Hollow out the bread, leaving a ½-inch-thick shell. (Cut the center into 1-inch cubes. Bake until toasted.)

With an electric mixer, beat the cream cheese, sour cream, cornstarch, and salsa together until smooth. Stir in the Cheddar cheese.

Spoon into the bread shell. Place the top of the bread back on. Wrap with foil.

Bake about 1 hour.

Serve with bread cubes and veggie sticks for dipping.

THICK AND CREAMY DIP

MAKES
ABOUT 1
CUP

0 GRAMS FAT

Prep :05
Cook :00
Stand 1:00
Total 1:05

^{1}/$_2$ cup fat-free sour cream
^{1}/$_2$ cup fat-free mayonnaise or salad dressing
1 tablespoon chopped chives
1^1/$_2$ teaspoons low-sodium Worcestershire sauce
^{1}/$_2$ teaspoon seasoned salt

Combine all ingredients, cover mixture, and chill for 1 hour. Serve with assorted fresh vegetables.

DILLED GARDEN DIP

MAKES
ABOUT
1^3/$_4$ cups

0 GRAMS FAT

Prep :10
Cook :05
Stand :00
Total :15

1^1/$_2$ cups no-fat cottage cheese
1 tablespoon lemon juice
1 tablespoon shredded carrot
1 tablespoon sliced green onion
1 tablespoon chopped fresh parsley
1^1/$_2$ teaspoons minced fresh dill weed, or ^{1}/$_2$ teaspoon dried
^{1}/$_2$ teaspoon sugar
Dash of pepper

In a blender, combine the cottage cheese and lemon juice and blend 3 to 5 minutes, or until smooth.

Spoon into a bowl and stir in the remaining ingredients.

Serve with raw vegetable sticks or Easy Tortilla Chips (see recipe on page 33).

FIESTA DIP

1 (8-ounce) package fat-free cream cheese, softened
1 (8-ounce) jar picante sauce
Green onions for garnish
Easy Tortilla Chips (see page 33)

MAKES 2
CUPS

0 GRAMS FAT

Combine cream cheese and picante sauce. Beat at low speed with an electric mixer until smooth. Garnish with thinly sliced green onions. Serve with tortilla chips for dipping.

Prep :05
Cook :00
Stand :00
Total :05

GUACAMOLE

1 small ripe avocado, peeled and pitted
2 medium tomatoes, chopped into small pieces
1/2 small red onion, chopped fine
4 teaspoons lime juice
1 clove garlic, chopped fine
1/2 small jalapeño pepper, seeded and chopped fine, or 1/4 cup salsa (see Note)

MAKES
ABOUT 2
CUPS

1 GRAM FAT
PER
TABLESPOON

Place the avocado in a large bowl and mash, not too fine—leave a little lumpy for texture. Add the remaining ingredients.

Note: These may be omitted if you do not desire the spicy Southwest bit.

Prep :10
Cook :00
Stand :00
Total :10

Tip: Save the avocado pit. If you push it into the center of your guacamole until ready to serve it will keep it from discoloring.

LAYERED TEX MEX DIP

SERVES 6

1 GRAM FAT

Prep :25
Cook :00
Stand :00
Total :25

1 (14-ounce) can chili beans, extra spicy, drained
1 (8-ounce) carton nonfat sour cream (1 cup)
1 tablespoon taco seasoning mix
2 (4-ounce) cans green chiles, drained
1 (16-ounce) package frozen peas, cooked
3 tablespoons lime juice
1 teaspoon minced garlic
4 ounces fat-free Cheddar cheese, shredded (1 cup)
1 teaspoon sliced green onion
1 cup finely chopped tomato
Easy Tortilla Chips (page 33)

In a blender, process the beans until smooth. Spread the bean mixture thinly on a large shallow platter.

In a small bowl, combine the sour cream and taco seasoning; blend well. Spread over the bean mixture; sprinkle with chiles.

In the blender combine the cooked peas, lime juice, and garlic. Process until smooth. Spread over the chiles.

Sprinkle with the cheese, green onion, and tomatoes. Serve with tortilla chips.

CHUNKY VEGETABLE SALSA

1 (8-ounce) can tomato juice
1 dash oregano
1 clove garlic, chopped fine, or dash of garlic seasoning
2 tablespoons vinegar
2 teaspoons lemon juice
2 teaspoons lime juice
2 rings jalapeño pepper, chopped fine
1 tablespoon cornstarch (optional)
2 (8-ounce) cans black-eyed peas, drained
2 large tomatoes, chopped
1 cup chopped celery
1 red onion, chopped
1 cup chopped green pepper
1 cup commercial salsa

SERVES 8

0 GRAMS FAT

Prep :15
Cook :03
Stand 1:00
Total 1:18

Combine the tomato juice, oregano, garlic, vinegar, lemon and lime juice, and jalapeño pepper in a small saucepan. Heat to boiling; thicken with a little cornstarch in cold water if desired. Pour over the peas, tomatoes, celery, onions, and pepper. Stir in the salsa. Refrigerate and let stand to blend at least 1 hour before serving.

Serve with chips or fat-free crackers.

SALSA VERDE

SERVES 4

0 GRAMS FAT

Prep :20
Cook :00
Stand :30
Total :50

2 cups chopped fresh or canned tomatoes
1/2 cup chopped onion
1/2 cup chopped cilantro or parsley
1 jalapeño pepper, canned or fresh, chopped
1 clove garlic, minced
1/2 teaspoon lemon pepper
1/2 teaspoon crushed oregano
1/2 teaspoon adobo seasoning or garlic powder
2 to 3 tablespoons lime juice

Combine all the ingredients in a medium bowl; mix well. Refrigerate at least 30 minutes to blend flavors. Serve with White Chicken Chili (page 76) or as a dip with tortilla chips.

ONION SALSA

SERVES 4

1 GRAM FAT
PER SERVING

Prep :10
Cook :00
Stand 2:00
Total 2:10

2 cups finely chopped red onion
1 tomato, chopped fine
1/4 cup chopped green onions
1/4 cup lemon juice
2 tablespoons chopped cilantro leaves
2 tablespoons wine vinegar
1 tablespoon canola oil
1 teaspoon reduced-sodium soy sauce
3 cloves garlic, chopped
1/4 teaspoon cayenne pepper

Mix all ingredients in a glass bowl, cover, and refrigerate at least 2 hours.

EASY TORTILLA CHIPS

12 (8-inch) flour tortillas

Heat the oven to 350 degrees. Cut each tortilla into 8 to 10 pie-shaped wedges. Place on an ungreased baking sheet in a single layer. Bake 10 to 15 minutes, or until golden brown. (Watch closely—they burn quickly.)

Variations: You can sprinkle the pieces with sugar and cinnamon before baking and eat as cookies. Try cocoa and sugar. Or try spicy chips—bar-b-q seasoning sprinkled over chips before baking, or garlic salt or Cajun seasoning.

MAKES ABOUT 96 CHIPS: 16 SERVINGS

1 GRAM FAT EACH TORTILLA (BEFORE CUTTING)

Prep :05
Cook :15
Stand :00
Total :20

PITA CHIPS

Fat-free.

4 (6-inch) whole wheat fat-free pita breads

Heat the oven to 400 degrees. Cut around the outside edges of the pitas to separate them, or slice them open to lay flat, so that you have 8 rounds. Cut each round into 8 pie-shaped wedges. Place in a single layer on a cookie sheet and bake until light brown and crispy.

MAKES 64 CHIPS (4 SERVINGS)

0 GRAMS FAT PER SERVING

Prep :05
Cook :12
Stand :00
Total :17

HAM APPETILLAS

SERVES 4

VERY LOW-FAT

Prep :15
Cook :00
Stand 3:00
Total 3:15

1 package flour tortillas
1 (8-ounce) package fat-free cream cheese, softened
$^{1}/_{3}$ cup fat-free mayonnaise
2 tablespoons chopped green onions
$^{1}/_{4}$ cup black olive pieces
4 to 5 slices ham, 98 percent fat-free

Let the tortillas sit at room temperature for a short while.

Combine the cream cheese, mayonnaise, onions, and olives until well mixed.

Spread a thin layer of the cheese mixture over each tortilla. Arrange a slice of ham over the cheese. Roll up the tortillas and wrap individually in plastic wrap.

Refrigerate at least 3 hours or overnight. To serve, cut into $^{3}/_{4}$-inch slices.

SKINNY PINWHEELS

SERVES 4

VERY LOW-FAT

Prep :10
Cook :00
Stand 2:00
Total 2:10

1 (8-ounce) package fat-free cream cheese, softened
1 (1-ounce) package ranch dressing mix
2 green onions, sliced
4 flour tortillas (each has 1 gram of fat)
1 (4-ounce) jar diced pimientos
1 (4-ounce) can chopped green chiles
1 (2-ounce) jar sliced black olives

Mix the cream cheese, ranch dressing mix, and green onions. Spread on the tortillas. Drain the pimientos, chiles, and olives and blot dry on a paper towel. Sprinkle in equal amounts on top of the cream cheese. Roll the tortillas tightly. Place seam side down in a dish and chill at least 2 hours.

Cut rolls into 1-inch pieces. Discard end pieces. (I eat them.) Serve with spiral side up.

STUFFED VEGETABLES WITH HERBED CREAM CHEESE

Vegetables for stuffing (cherry tomatoes, celery stalks, hollowed-out cucumber
  chunks, mushroom caps, etc.)
1 (8-ounce) package fat-free cream cheese, softened
$^1/_3$ cup grated fat-free Parmesan cheese
1 teaspoon skim milk
$^1/_2$ teaspoon Italian herb seasoning
$^1/_8$ teaspoon black pepper

LESS THAN 1
GRAM FAT

Prep :10
Cook :10
Stand :00
Total :20

Prepare veggies of your choice.

In a small bowl mix the cream cheese, Parmesan, milk, season-ing, and pepper. With a pastry bag, fill vegetables.

(You can put the filling into a zipper bag and cut the corner off to use as a pastry bag.)

Serve chilled.

POTATO SKINS

*Fat-free sour cream or sour cream dip or
salsa makes a nice dip for these.*

6 medium baking potatoes, scrubbed, baked, and cooled (may be leftovers or
  extras baked the day before)
4 to 6 tablespoons Butter Buds, liquid form
$^1/_2$ teaspoon garlic powder
Black pepper to taste

SERVES 12

0.06 GRAMS
FAT PER
SERVING

Prep :15
Cook :20
Stand :00
Total :35

Preheat the oven to 450 degrees.

Cut each potato in half. Scoop out the centers, leaving about $^1/_4$ inch of potato on the inside of each skin. Save the centers for another recipe another day. Cut the skins into quarters. Brush

Butter Buds over the inside and sprinkle with garlic powder and pepper. Place skin side down on a baking sheet.

Bake 15 minutes, or until lightly browned. Turn skins over and bake another 5 minutes. Serve immediately.

Variations: Instead of garlic powder, use Cajun seasoning, onion flakes, onion soup mix, or your choice of seasoning.

CHICKEN-STUFFED MUSHROOMS

SERVES 12

1 GRAM FAT
EACH

Prep :15
Cook :10
Stand :00
Total :25

1 small onion, chopped
2 tablespoons cilantro leaves
2 tablespoons egg substitute
1 tablespoon Dijon mustard
1¹/₂ teaspoons finely chopped fresh ginger root
2 tablespoons reduced-sodium soy sauce
1 clove garlic, chopped fine
¹/₂ pound ground raw chicken
12 large mushrooms, stems removed

Preheat the oven to 350 degrees. Spray a cookie sheet with vegetable oil cooking spray. Mix all ingredients except mushrooms. Fill mushrooms with the chicken mixture. Place the mushrooms, filled sides up, on the cookie sheet and bake for 10 to 15 minutes, or until chicken mixture is done. Serve hot.

Broiled Mushroom Caps: Brush stuffed mushrooms with Butter Buds or spray with vegetable oil cooking spray, and bake at 400 degrees for 5 to 10 minutes.

Soups and Salads

Soups

VEGETABLE SOUP

FAT-FREE

Prep :15
Cook 4:30
Stand 8:00
Total 12:45

Cook beef the day before. Any cut will do but trim all the fat possible off. Put beef and soup bones in a large pot and cover with cold water. Simmer 3 to 4 hours. Defat broth. Refrigerate overnight to collect any excess fat missed. Dip the fat off the top before starting the soup. Save the beef for another dish another day.

Bring broth to a boil. Add 2 medium onions, chopped; 1 clove of garlic, minced; celery, carrots, potatoes, peas (as much as your family prefers), 2 cans tomatoes, spices as you desire. Cabbage may also be added. Simmer all the ingredients slowly for about 1½ to 2 hours. Pasta may also be added if desired.

Season with Herbs to Add Flavor
Fat is flavor. When you take out the fat, you need to add more herbs to enhance the flavor.
Caraway—tangy and slightly sweet
Cardamom—spicy
Celery—strong—be careful
Cumin—a little bitter and sometimes hot
Dill—strong—use sparingly
Fennel—licorice flavor
Mustard—spicy
Sesame—sweet nutty flavor

Be very careful to serve your hot soup *hot* and your cold soup *cold*. A quick way to ruin the taste of an effort-filled soup is to serve it warm.

BEAN SOUP

2 cups dried navy or pea beans
Defatted ham broth or water
1 small onion, chopped fine
1/2 cup chopped celery
Salt and pepper to taste

SERVES 6

0 GRAMS FAT

Prep :10
Cook 1:30
Stand 8:00
Total 9:40

Soak the beans overnight in 6 cups of water in a large kettle. Drain, cover with defatted ham broth, and bring to a boil. Lower the heat and simmer, partially covered, for about 1 hour, or until almost tender.

Add the onion, celery, salt, and pepper, and continue cooking until beans are tender and liquid is thick. Mash about ³/₄ of the beans with a potato masher and continue to simmer for a short while until very thick. (Careful, or they will scorch!) Taste the soup and add additional salt and pepper if needed.

Variation: The soup may be thickened with mashed potatoes if you are rushed for time or have the potatoes on hand.

HEALTHY HEARTY POTATO SOUP

6 medium potatoes
2 carrots
6 stalks celery
2 quarts water
1 onion, chopped
6 tablespoons light margarine
6 tablespoons flour
1 teaspoon salt
1/2 teaspoon pepper
1 1/2 cups skim milk

SERVES 8

LESS THAN 1
GRAM FAT PER
SERVING

Prep :10
Cook :45
Stand :00
Total :55

Peel and slice the potatoes, dice the carrots and celery, cover with 2 quarts or so of water, and cook until tender, 30 to 40 minutes. Drain, reserving the liquid and setting the vegetables aside.

In the same kettle, sauté the onion in margarine until soft. Stir in the flour, salt, and pepper. Gradually add milk and cook until thickened, about 5 minutes. Stir in the cooked vegetables carefully so as not to smash them. Add 1 cup or more of reserved cooking liquid until soup is desired consistency.

CREAMY POTATO CABBAGE SOUP

SERVES 5

0 GRAMS FAT

Prep :10
Cook :45
Stand :00
Total :55

3 medium potatoes, peeled and cubed
1 (14-ounce) can fat-free chicken broth
$^{1}/_{2}$ cup skim milk
2 cups shredded cabbage
$^{1}/_{2}$ cup diced carrots
$^{1}/_{2}$ teaspoon dried dill weed

Combine the potatoes with the broth in a saucepan. Bring to a boil. Reduce the heat and cook until the potatoes are tender, about 40 minutes. Cool slightly.

Place 1 cup of the hot potato mixture in a blender or food processor. Add the milk, mix until smooth, return to the saucepan, and stir in remaining ingredients. Cook for 5 to 7 minutes, or until the carrots and cabbage are crisp-tender.

Thicken your soup with flour, cornstarch, or mashed potatoes. It's better to remove the pan from the heat before adding your thickeners to avoid the danger of lumping. Cornstarch is better for soups to be served cold and flour for hot soups. Leftover mashed potatoes thicken bean, potato, or any cream-type soup nicely.

POTATO SOUP

3 or 4 large potatoes
1 medium onion
3 cups skim milk
¹/₄ cup Butter Buds
Salt and pepper to taste

SERVES 4

0 GRAMS FAT

Peel and dice potatoes and onion, cover with water, and bring to a boil. Lower the heat and cook until tender, about 35 minutes.

Drain three quarters of the water off and add the milk. Simmer over low heat for 15 to 20 minutes. Mash the potatoes with a hand masher to make the soup thicken. Add the Butter Buds, salt, and pepper.

Serve with fat-free soda crackers.

Prep :10
Cook :50
Stand :00
Total 1:00

Salads

GREEN SALAD

SERVES 4

1 GRAM FAT
PER SERVING

Prep :15
Cook :00
Stand :00
Total :15

1 head lettuce, cleaned and torn into bite-size pieces
1 tomato, chopped
1 small green bell pepper, seeded and chopped
2 stalks celery, chopped
2 cups white seedless grapes
1 avocado, peeled, seeded, and diced
Fat-free ranch dressing

Put the lettuce in a bowl and top with the tomato, bell pepper, celery, grapes, and avocado. Toss lightly with the dressing just before serving.

SPINACH-ORANGE SALAD

SERVES 2

1 GRAM FAT
PER SERVING

Prep :15
Cook :00
Stand 3:00
Total 3:15

2 teaspoons canola oil
$^1/_2$ teaspoon crumbled marjoram
Pinch of black pepper
Pinch of nutmeg
2 cups coarsely chopped orange sections
2 medium-size radishes, trimmed and sliced thin
1 green onion, top and all, chopped
$^1/_2$ pound fresh spinach, trimmed
1$^1/_4$ teaspoons rice vinegar or white wine vinegar

Combine the oil, marjoram, pepper, and nutmeg in a serving bowl. Add the orange sections, radishes, and green onion. Toss well. Cover and chill in refrigerator for 2 to 3 hours, tossing occasionally.

Wash and pat dry the spinach. Tear into bite-size pieces. Just before serving, add the spinach and vinegar to the chilled ingredients and toss well.

COLESLAW

Dressing:
3 tablespoons plain nonfat yogurt
2 tablespoons nonfat sour cream
$^3/_4$ teaspoon prepared yellow mustard
$^1/_2$ teaspoon sugar
$^1/_2$ teaspoon cider vinegar
$^1/_4$ teaspoon celery seed
$^1/_8$ teaspoon salt
$^1/_8$ teaspoon pepper

1$^3/_4$ cups shredded cabbage

SERVES 2

0 GRAMS FAT

Prep :15
Cook :00
Stand 3:00
Total 3:15

Mix dressing ingredients and add to cabbage. Toss well. Cover and refrigerate 2 to 3 hours, stirring occasionally.

To make your cabbage crisp, soak the cabbage head, cut in half, in salted water for about 1 hour. Drain well before chopping.

OVERNIGHT SLAW

SERVES 4

0 GRAMS FAT

Prep :20
Cook :00
Stand 8:00
Total 8:20

4 cups shredded cabbage
¹/₄ cup thinly sliced purple onion rings
³/₄ cup sugar
³/₄ cup white vinegar
³/₄ cup water
2 teaspoons salt

   Combine the cabbage and onion in a large bowl. Mix the sugar, vinegar, water, and salt, stirring until the sugar dissolves. Pour over the cabbage mixture and toss gently. Cover and chill 8 hours or overnight. Serve with a slotted spoon.

APPLE-CARROT SLAW

SERVES 6

0.3 GRAMS FAT

Prep :20
Cook :00
Stand :45
Total 1:05

1 medium cabbage, shredded (about 4 cups)
1³/₄ cups shredded carrots
1³/₄ cups chopped unpeeled red apple
²/₃ cup fat-free mayonnaise
2 tablespoons sugar
¹/₃ cup white vinegar
1 teaspoon celery seed

   Combine the cabbage, carrots, and apple in a large bowl. Mix the mayonnaise with the sugar, vinegar, and celery seed. Pour over the cabbage. Toss gently to coat. Cover and chill 45 minutes or longer before serving.

CUCUMBER STORY

I live in farm country, am a farmer's daughter, farmer's sister, farmer's aunt. You think that you know a little about farming after so many years, *but* . . . A couple years ago there was a nice man who came into this area wanting some of the farmers to put in cucumbers. Cucumbers had never been grown here on a large scale before, so a challenge was in the air.

After many meetings, much planning, and several months, the cucumber crop was planted. My brother was one of the experimenting farmers.

The nice man and his wife were in this area just at planting, cultivating, and harvest times. They needed a place to stay; we have a little guest house that we rent; so they rented it. He is the type of man who has a contagious smile, an apple-pie boy-next-door face, and a sweet personality, so I nicknamed him "Sweetie." Being the type of man he is, he was rather embarrassed by this name, which just made it much more fun for me as I am rather ornery. He has a car phone in his pickup truck, and when I needed to phone him I always said, "Sweetie," so that all of the farmers in the bottom would become acquainted with his name. Ha. He wanted to kill me! OK, we became the best of friends.

He was referred to in the area by all of the farmers as the Pickle Man. They were even introduced in church as Mr. and Mrs. Pickle Man. That makes him even more special—he is a good Christian man.

The story of the cucumbers is very interesting. Did you know that when they start to bloom you have to have hives of bees brought in and placed all around the field so they can pollinate them? I thought that was very interesting. The pickers are big machines like harvesters that pick them vine and all. They separate the cukes from the vines and dump them in a hopper.

These people did not bother to tell all of us in this area about the bees. We went over to pick some cukes one day and guess what? Bees all over us—in the truck, on our clothes, in our hair. One guy got his truck used as a hive and had to leave it there until they moved. We soon learned not to leave the window down on your truck.

The cucumbers were not too successful in this area—too many weather difficulties, I suppose. But that was quite a summer, having the cukes, bees, and Sweetie around for a few months. Sweetie and I are still the best of friends, as are he and my husband. They really liked to go fishing together. They live in Missouri but we all still keep in touch. You meet some of the nicest people in some of the strangest situations at the oddest times. Meet all of the nice people you can. You never know when there is a Sweetie just around the corner.

I made every kind of pickle I could think of that summer, and made up all kinds of dishes using cucumbers. Whatever is on hand is what you try to use. Try the Creamy Cucumbers. I did *not* try cucumber pie; I will leave that to you to do.

CREAMY CUCUMBERS

SERVES 2

0 GRAMS FAT

Prep :10
Cook :00
Stand 4:00
Total 4:10

¹/₂ cup plain nonfat yogurt
¹/₂ teaspoon salt
¹/₄ teaspoon dill weed
2 cups thinly sliced cucumbers
1 small onion, sliced thin and separated into rings
Lettuce Leaves

Mix all ingredients, cover, and refrigerate at least 4 hours

FESTIVE CORN SALAD

1 (12-ounce) can white whole-kernel corn, drained and rinsed
1 medium green pepper, seeded and chopped
1 medium tomato, chopped
1 medium purple onion, chopped
¹/₄ teaspoon pepper
¹/₂ cup commercial fat-free Italian salad dressing
Lettuce leaves

SERVES 2

0 GRAMS FAT

Prep :15
Cook :00
Stand :00
Total :15

Combine all ingredients. Toss lightly. Serve on lettuce leaves.

Variation: Fat-free mayonnaise may be substituted for Italian dressing.

CORN AND TOMATO SALAD

¹/₄ cup plain nonfat yogurt
2 tablespoons ketchup
1 teaspoon prepared mustard
2 green onions, including tops, chopped
2 tablespoons snipped fresh dill or ¹/₂ teaspoon dried dill weed
2 cups fresh or frozen whole-kernel corn
10 cherry tomatoes, halved
1 small green pepper, chopped
Lettuce leaves

SERVES 1

0 GRAMS FAT

Prep :10
Cook :01
Stand :00
Total :11

Combine the yogurt, ketchup, and mustard in a serving bowl; stir in the green onions and dill. Set the dressing aside.

Bring 2 cups of water to a boil, add the corn, and cook 1 minute, or just until tender. Drain in a colander. Rinse with cold water to stop the cooking and drain again.

Add the corn to the yogurt dressing along with the tomatoes and green pepper. Mix well. Serve on lettuce leaves.

POTATO SALAD

SERVES 8

0 GRAMS FAT

Prep :25
Cook :30
Stand 1:00
Total 1:55

Salad:
4 to 5 large potatoes
1 cup chopped celery
1 cup chopped onion
³/₄ cup chopped green pepper
³/₄ cup chopped dill or sweet pickles

Dressing:
1 cup fat-free mayonnaise (or more, depending on amount of potatoes)
2 to 3 tablespoons mustard
3 tablespoons pickle juice
Touch of salt
Pepper to taste

Boil the potatoes in their skins in water to cover for 30 minutes or until tender. When they are cool enough to handle, peel them and cut into cubes. Mix with the celery, onion, green pepper, and pickles and place in a large bowl.

Mix the dressing ingredients, pour over the salad, and toss gently. Refrigerate at least 1 hour before serving.

Variation: To do a day ahead: Layer vegetables in the bowl, potatoes on top. Do *not* stir. Cover and refrigerate. Mix the dressing, cover, and store. Combine the salad and dressing at least 1 hour before serving.

HOT POTATO SALAD

4 to 5 cups thinly sliced potatoes
³/₄ cup chopped onion
1 tablespoon fat-free margarine or Butter Buds
¹/₂ cup fat-free mayonnaise
¹/₃ cup apple cider vinegar
1 tablespoon sugar
Salt and pepper to taste
Chopped parsley (optional)

SERVES 6

0 GRAMS FAT

Prep :10
Cook :25
Stand :00
Total :35

Cover potatoes with cold water, bring to a boil, and cook 15 to 20 minutes, until just tender—do *not* overcook. Drain and set aside.

Sauté the onion in ¹/₄ cup water in a nonstick skillet 3 to 5 minutes, until tender-crisp. Add the margarine, and stir until melted. Combine the mayonnaise, vinegar, sugar, salt, and pepper with the onion mixture. Add potatoes and place the skillet over low heat, stirring constantly until heated. Sprinkle with parsley if desired.

GERMAN POTATO SALAD

4 medium potatoes
¹/₃ cup vinegar
1 tablespoon sugar
2 teaspoons flour
¹/₄ teaspoon pepper
1 onion, chopped
³/₄ cup chopped celery
1 green pepper, seeded and chopped
2 hard-cooked eggs (discard yolks—bad!), chopped
2 tablespoons low-fat bacon bits

SERVES 4

LESS THAN 1
GRAM FAT

Prep :25
Cook :35
Stand :10
Total 1:10

Boil the potatoes in water to cover for 30 to 35 minutes, or until tender. Drain. When cool enough to handle, peel them and cut into small cubes. Set aside.

In a heavy saucepan combine the vinegar, sugar, flour, and pepper with ½ cup of water. Whisk over medium heat until the dressing just comes to a boil (2 to 3 minutes).

Combine the potatoes, onion, celery, and green pepper in a serving bowl. Pour the hot dressing over and toss well. Cool to room temperature. When ready to serve, garnish with the chopped egg whites and bacon bits.

POTATO-GREEN PEA SALAD

SERVES 6

0 GRAMS FAT

Prep :25
Cook :40
Stand 1:00
Total 2:05

Salad:
4 to 5 medium potatoes
2 cups frozen green peas, thawed
1 cup chopped celery
¼ cup sliced green onions
¼ cup chopped green pepper

Dressing:
½ cup fat-free mayonnaise
½ cup plain nonfat yogurt
1 to 2 tablespoons prepared mustard
1 teaspoon vinegar
Salt and pepper to taste

Boil the potatoes in water to cover for 30 to 40 minutes, or until tender. When cool enough to handle, peel them and cut into cubes. You should have about 7 cups.

Combine the potatoes with the rest of the salad ingredients in a serving bowl.

Mix the dressing ingredients and pour over the salad mixture. Toss lightly. Refrigerate at least 1 hour before serving.

Variation: A good do-ahead recipe. Layer the salad ingredients, peas on bottom and potatoes on top. Cover and refrigerate. Combine the dressing ingredients, cover, and refrigerate. Toss together lightly at least 1 hour before serving.

LACY WALDORF SALAD

Salad:
$^3/_4$ medium head lettuce, chopped fine
$^3/_4$ cup white grapes, halved
$^1/_4$ cup chopped celery
1 sliced green onion
$^1/_2$ cup chopped pecans
1 apple, peeled and chopped

Dressing:
1 cup fat-free salad dressing, such as Miracle Whip
2 tablespoons lemon juice
1 tablespoon sugar
2 tablespoons skim milk

SERVES 4

0 GRAMS FAT
IF PECANS
OMITTED

Prep :15
Cook :00
Stand :00
Total :15

Combine the salad ingredients in a large bowl. Blend the dressing ingredients until smooth. Pour over the salad and toss to combine.

Variation: To make your salad prettier when having company, divide the salad between 4 chilled salad plates and lay a very thin slice of avocado on the side of each salad dish.

LAYERED MEXICAN GARDEN SALAD

SERVES 2

LESS THAN
1 GRAM FAT
PER SERVING

Prep :10
Cook :00
Stand :00
Total :10

The amount of ingredients depends on how many salads you want to make. This is for two.

Shredded lettuce
1 (16-ounce) can pinto beans in Mexican-style sauce, drained
1 cup chopped zucchini
1 cup chopped tomato
$1/4$ cup chopped onion
$1/2$ cup thick and chunky salsa, or as needed
4 ounces shredded fat-free Cheddar cheese
Red or green chile peppers

Line individual salad plates with lettuce. Cover with a layer of beans, then with layers of zucchini, tomato, and onion. Spoon salsa evenly over the vegetables (more may be added if desired). Sprinkle with cheese. Garnish with red or green chile peppers if desired.

COTTAGE CHEESE SALAD

SERVES 2

0 GRAMS FAT

Prep :10
Cook :00
Stand 1:00
Total 1:10

2 Roma tomatoes, or 1 large tomato, chopped
2 green onions, chopped
2 cups fat-free cottage cheese
Salt and pepper

Mix the chopped tomatoes and onions with the cottage cheese. Let stand about 1 hour to blend flavors. Salt and pepper to taste before serving.

TABBOULEH

1 cup bulgur or cracked wheat
2 cups boiling water
4 teaspoons lemon juice
2 teaspoons olive oil
2 medium ripe tomatoes, chopped
3 tablespoons minced parsley
$^1/_2$ small red onion, chopped
2 green onions, including tops, chopped fine
$^1/_4$ teaspoon ground coriander
$^1/_4$ teaspoon ground cumin
$^1/_8$ teaspoon hot pepper sauce
Lettuce leaves

SERVES 2

1 GRAM FAT
PER $^3/_4$-CUP
SERVING

Prep :20
Cook :00
Stand :30
Total :50

Place bulgur in a large bowl and pour boiling water over. Cover and let stand for 30 minutes. Drain off any liquid that remains.

In another bowl mix the lemon juice, olive oil, tomatoes, parsley, red and green onions, and seasonings. Add the bulgur and toss well to mix. Serve on lettuce leaves.

QUICK PASTA SALAD

Salad:
2 cups pasta, cooked and drained
1 cup frozen green peas, rinsed in hot water and drained
2 cups frozen stir-fry vegetables, rinsed in hot water and drained

Dressing:
$^3/_4$ cup fat-free mayonnaise
$^1/_4$ cup fat-free Italian salad dressing

SERVES 6

0 GRAMS FAT

Prep :05
Cook :00
Stand :00
Total :05

Put the salad ingredients in a serving bowl. Combine the dressing ingredients, mix well, and add to the salad. Toss until combined.

> I keep a package of frozen stir-fry vegetables in the freezer at all times for rush jobs like the Quick Pasta Salad. This is good for ladies who work and are always in a hurry.

MACARONI SALAD

**SERVES
6 TO 8**

0 GRAMS FAT

Prep :30
Cook :25
Stand :30
Total 1:25

1 (8-ounce) package of macaroni, any style or shape desired
1 large tomato, diced
³/₄ cup chopped onion
³/₄ cup chopped green pepper
³/₄ cup pimiento-stuffed green olives, sliced
1 cup fat-free mayonnaise (approximately)
Salt and pepper

Cook the macaroni in a large pot of boiling water until tender but still firm. Drain in a colander; rinse with cold water and drain thoroughly.

In a large bowl, combine the macaroni with the tomato, onion, green pepper, and olives. Toss lightly.

Add enough fat-free mayonnaise to desired moistness. Salt and pepper to taste. Mix well. Chill for 30 minutes before serving.

Variation: A good do-ahead dish: Layer the ingredients in a serving dish, starting with tomatoes on the bottom; this keeps any juice from making other items soggy. Put the drained macaroni on top and seal with plastic wrap. The dressing should be added about ½ hour before serving time so flavors may blend. Drain any excess juice off before adding dressing.

Salad Dressings

CREAMY SALAD DRESSING

1 cup fat-free salad dressing, such as Miracle Whip
1 cup fat-free ranch dressing
1 tablespoon lemon juice
1 tablespoon sugar
$^1/_4$ cup skim milk

Mix all ingredients with a wire whisk until smooth. Serve over your favorite salad greens or fruit.

MAKES
ABOUT
2$^1/_4$ CUPS

0 GRAMS FAT

Prep :05
Cook :00
Stand :00
Total :05

CREAMY GARLIC DRESSING

$^1/_2$ cup skim milk
2 tablespoons lemon juice
1 tablespoon canola oil
1$^1/_2$ cups fat-free cottage cheese, drained
$^1/_4$ cup chopped onion
2 cloves garlic, chopped fine
$^1/_2$ teaspoon salt
$^1/_4$ teaspoon pepper
$^1/_4$ teaspoon paprika

Combine all the ingredients and mix well. Store in a covered container in the refrigerator at least 1 hour before using.

MAKES
ABOUT 2
CUPS

1 GRAM FAT
PER SERVING

Prep :10
Cook :00
Stand 1:00
Total 1:10

CREAMY COLESLAW DRESSING

MAKES ⅓
CUP

0 GRAMS FAT

Prep :05
Cook :00
Stand 1:00
Total 1:05

½ cup plain nonfat yogurt
2 tablespoons Dijon mustard
1 tablespoon fat-free mayonnaise
2 teaspoons sugar
Pepper and salt to taste

Mix all ingredients. To serve, pour over shredded cabbage and refrigerate at least 1 hour.

HONEY MUSTARD DRESSING

MAKES
ABOUT 1½
CUPS

0 GRAMS FAT

Prep :10
Cook :00
Stand 1:00
Total 1:10

½ cup lemon juice
¼ cup honey
2 tablespoons prepared mustard
1 teaspoon salt
½ teaspoon paprika
2 cloves garlic, chopped fine
⅔ cup water

Mix all the ingredients and shake well. Store in a covered container at least 1 hour before serving.

Poultry

Chicken

POT ROASTED CHICKEN

SERVES 6

2 GRAMS FAT
PER SERVING

Prep :15
Cook :45
Stand :00
Total 1:00

1 chicken, cut up and skinned (or use only breast, for less fat)
7 or 8 small new potatoes, scrubbed
4 or 5 small onions, peeled
4 medium carrots, peeled and cut into 3-inch pieces
$^1/_2$ cup dry white wine
1 (14-ounce) can low-fat reduced-sodium chicken broth
1 tablespoon lemon juice
3 cloves garlic, chopped fine
1 teaspoon oregano
$^1/_2$ teaspoon thyme
$^1/_4$ teaspoon black pepper
2 tablespoons chopped parsley

Preheat the oven to 350 degrees.

Arrange the chicken, potatoes, onions, and carrots in a baking dish.

Mix the wine, broth, and lemon juice. Pour over chicken and vegetables.

Sprinkle on garlic, oregano, thyme, and pepper.

Bake uncovered 40 to 45 minutes or until chicken is fork tender. Turn veggies and chicken occasionally and baste with pan juices. (If juices evaporate too quickly, add more chicken broth.)

Transfer to a serving platter, arranging vegetables around chicken, and sprinkle with parsley.

Tip: Dark meat is fattier than white meat. Ounce for ounce drumsticks have more than twice the fat of chicken breasts.

LEMON HONEY GLAZE FOR BAKED CHICKEN

Dresses up a plain baked chicken to taste like Sunday Company's A Comin'.

MAKES ½ CUP

0 GRAMS FAT

Prep :05
Cook :00
Stand :00
Total :05

¹/₄ cup lemon juice
¹/₄ cup honey
1 teaspoon chopped parsley

Mix the above ingredients and brush over chicken when about ²/₃ of the way done when baking.

Lemon Honey Glazed Pork: Spoon some glaze over lean pork chops for the final 10 minutes of cooking.

DRESSING PAN

I have this neat old pan that is my dressing pan. I bet many of you have just such a pan. Mine belonged to my grandmother. My mom had it for many years; I kept borrowing it and finally forgot to take it home. She fussed so that one year I wrapped it up and gave it to her for a Christmas gift. Years later she gave it back to me because I now do all the dressing baking in our family.

Mom is a retired dressing maker. There always seems to be one person in each family that tackles the dressing. This pan is an old beat-up round, deep, ugly pan. I bet you know exactly what I am talking about. Sounds just like that one in your cabinet that you always drag out for dressing, doesn't it? I hope someday my granddaughter will be making dressing in this pan. Dressing day is such a special day with most families, make each one special.

CORN BREAD DRESSING

SERVES 8

VERY LOW-FAT

Prep :15
Cook :40
Stand :00
Total :55

1 recipe Corn Bread (page 151), made a day ahead
2 cups chopped onions
2 cups chopped celery
2 to 4 tablespoons sage (some like a stronger sage taste)
2 cups defatted chicken stock (use more if desired)
Salt and pepper to taste
³/₄ cup egg substitute
Butter Buds

Crumble cold corn bread into a bowl. Add the onions, celery, sage, chicken stock, salt, pepper, and egg substitute. Mix well. Pour into a baking dish that has been coated with vegetable oil cooking spray. Bake in a preheated 350 degree oven for 30 minutes. Pour Butter Buds over the top, as if dotting with butter. Continue baking until desired doneness.

Variation: I cook my onions and celery until crisp tender and use some of the water they were cooked in to help moisten the dressing and give it a nice flavor.

Baked Chicken and Dressing: Boil some boneless, skinless chicken breasts while mixing this. Cut them up into bite-size pieces and place on top of the dressing. Push down just enough to cover the chicken. This keeps it from drying out, and you now have chicken and dressing that looks like you have worked for hours preparing. Don't say a word!

PICANTE CHICKEN WITH BROWN RICE

$^3/_4$ pound boneless, skinless chicken breasts, cut into strips
$1^1/_2$ teaspoons chili powder
1 teaspoon ground cumin
$^1/_4$ cup cold water
$^1/_2$ cup sliced green onions
2 cloves garlic, chopped fine
1 (14-ounce) can whole tomatoes, undrained and cut up
1 cup frozen corn kernels
$^3/_4$ cup uncooked instant brown rice
2 tablespoons chopped green chiles, undrained
$^1/_2$ cup water

SERVES 2

3 GRAMS FAT
PER SERVING

Prep :10
Cook :25
Stand :00
Total :35

Heat a nonstick skillet; add the chicken and sprinkle with chili powder and cumin. Add $^1/_4$ cup water, the green onions, and garlic. Sauté until the chicken is no longer pink.

Stir in the tomatoes, corn, rice, chiles, and $^1/_2$ cup water. Bring to a boil. Reduce the heat, cover, and simmer 5 to 10 minutes, or until the rice is done.

PARMESAN CHICKEN

SERVES 6

2 GRAMS FAT PER SERVING

Prep :10
Cook :30
Stand :00
Total :40

6 boneless, skinless chicken breast halves
2 tablespoons fat-free margarine, melted
$^1/_2$ cup grated fat-free Parmesan cheese (see Note)
$^1/_4$ cup dry bread crumbs
1 teaspoon oregano
1 teaspoon parsley
$^1/_4$ teaspoon paprika
Salt and pepper to taste

Heat the oven to 400 degrees. Spray a baking dish with vegetable oil cooking spray.

Dip the chicken in the melted margarine (use liquid Butter Buds if you prefer). Combine the remaining ingredients and coat the chicken with the crumb mixture. Place in the baking dish and bake uncovered for 25 to 30 minutes, or until tender and golden brown.

Note: Weight Watchers makes a fat-free Parmesan.

CHICKEN DIJON

SERVES 4

ULTRA LOW-FAT

Prep :10
Cook 1:00
Stand :00
Total 1:10

$^1/_2$ cup fat-free salad dressing, such as Miracle Whip
$^1/_4$ cup Dijon mustard
4 to 6 boneless, skinless chicken breast halves
1$^1/_4$ cups dry bread crumbs, fat-free
$^1/_4$ cup Butter Buds, liquid form

Preheat the oven to 350 degrees.

Combine salad dressing and mustard, blending well. Brush chicken with the mixture and coat with crumbs. Place in a baking dish that has been coated with vegetable oil cooking spray. Drizzle with Butter Buds.

Bake uncovered for 45 minutes to 1 hour, or until chicken is done to desired tenderness.

CHICKEN CORDON BLEU

8 boneless, skinless chicken breast halves
$^1/_4$ cup chopped parsley
4 ounces fat-free mozzarella cheese, sliced
4 slices low-fat ham
$^3/_4$ cup egg substitute
1 cup seasoned bread crumbs
White Wine Sauce (recipe follows)
1 tablespoon minced fresh parsley

SERVES 8

4 GRAMS FAT
PER SERVING

Prep :25
Cook :35
Stand :00
Total 1:00

Preheat the oven to 400 degrees.

Pound the chicken breast pieces until they are thin. Sprinkle with parsley. Top each piece with a thin layer of cheese, then a half slice of ham. Roll up tightly.

Roll each breast in egg substitute and coat with bread crumbs. Spray a baking dish with cooking spray. Arrange chicken rolls in the dish with the seam sides down (secure with a toothpick if desired).

Bake for 30 minutes, or until browned and cooked through. Pour a small amount of White Wine Sauce over each chicken breast when served and sprinkle with parsley.

WHITE WINE SAUCE

MAKES
ABOUT
3½ CUPS

2 cups fat-free chicken broth
½ cup white wine
6 tablespoons all-purpose flour
¾ cup skim milk
Onion powder and pepper to taste (optional)

LOW-FAT

Prep :05
Cook :10
Stand :00
Total :15

Combine the broth and wine in a nonstick saucepan. Heat to boiling; reduce heat. Mix flour and milk in a small cup until smooth; stir into broth. Cook and stir until mixture is thick. Thin with a little water if necessary. Add onion powder and pepper if desired.

"FRIED" CORNMEAL-COATED CHICKEN

SERVES 6

Nice and brown, this chicken gives you the fried satisfaction without the fatisfaction.

2 GRAMS FAT
PER SERVING

Prep :10
Cook :40
Stand :00
Total :50

1 cup cornmeal
¼ teaspoon oregano
½ teaspoon chili powder
6 boneless, skinless chicken breast halves

Preheat the oven to 350 degrees. Mix the cornmeal, oregano, and chili powder. Coat the chicken with the cornmeal mixture. Arrange the pieces in a baking dish that has been coated with cooking spray. Spray the tops lightly with cooking spray. Bake, without turning, until tender, about 30 to 45 minutes.

Serve with salsa or ketchup.

CHEESY OAT-BAKED CHICKEN

2 cups quick-cooking oats
$^1/_4$ cup fat-free Parmesan cheese
1 teaspoon paprika
$^1/_2$ teaspoon pepper
6 boneless, skinless chicken breast halves
2 egg whites or egg substitute

SERVES 6

2 GRAMS FAT
PER SERVING

Prep :15
Cook :40
Stand :00
Total :55

Preheat the oven to 350 degrees. Spray a 13 x 9 x 2-inch baking pan with cooking spray. Combine the oats, Parmesan, paprika, and pepper. Dip the chicken in the egg whites; coat with the oat mixture. Arrange the chicken pieces in the prepared pan; spray lightly with cooking spray. Bake uncovered until tender, approximately 30 to 45 minutes.

CHICKEN CREOLE

1 medium onion, chopped
1 medium bell pepper, seeded and chopped
1 stalk celery, chopped
2 cloves garlic, chopped fine
2 whole chicken breasts, halved and skinned
1 teaspoon paprika
$^1/_2$ teaspoon cayenne pepper
1 (12-ounce) can low-sodium stewed tomatoes
1 teaspoon dried rosemary
$^1/_2$ teaspoon dried marjoram
1 bay leaf
1 tablespoon flour
$^1/_4$ cup defatted chicken broth or water

SERVES 4

2 GRAMS FAT
PER SERVING

Prep :15
Cook :45
Stand :00
Total 1:00

Sauté the onion, pepper, celery, and garlic in $^1/_4$ cup water in a medium-size skillet. (If using frozen onions and peppers you don't need to use any water; enough will cook out of them to do the job.)

Sauté until the onion is just tender, about 3 minutes. Transfer to a small dish.

Sprinkle the chicken with paprika and cayenne pepper. Put the chicken in the skillet and cook about 5 minutes, turning occasionally.

Add half the cooked vegetables to the skillet along with tomatoes, rosemary, marjoram, and bay leaf. Reduce the heat, cover, and simmer for 20 to 25 minutes, or until fork tender.

Dissolve the flour in the chicken broth. Stir into the pan juices and cook, stirring constantly, until thickened. Add the reserved cooked vegetables and heat for 3 to 4 minutes. Discard bay leaf. Serve with rice and steamed okra.

MUSHROOM DILL CHICKEN

SERVES 4

2 GRAMS FAT
EACH

Prep :20
Cook :40
Stand :00
Total 1:00

4 boneless, skinless chicken breast halves
2 tablespoons Butter Buds, liquid form
1 cup hot water
2 cups Stove Top stuffing, chicken flavor
1 green or red bell pepper (optional), seeded and chopped fine
$^{1}/_{4}$ cup egg substitute
Pepper to taste
1 (10$^{3}/_{4}$-ounce) can Healthy Request cream of mushroom soup
$^{1}/_{2}$ teaspoon dried dill weed

Preheat the oven to 350 degrees. Lay the chicken breast halves on a flat surface and pound with a rolling pin or meat mallet to $^{1}/_{4}$-inch thickness.

Combine the Butter Buds, hot water, stuffing mix, chopped bell pepper if using, and egg substitute. Mix until moistened. Spoon evenly over the chicken. Roll up tightly, starting with a long end. Secure with toothpicks. Place seam side down in a square baking dish that has been sprayed with vegetable oil cooking spray. Spray the chicken lightly and sprinkle with pepper.

Bake uncovered, without turning, until tender, about 30 to 40 minutes. Heat the soup with ½ cup water and the dill in a saucepan. Serve spooned over the chicken.

QUICK CHICKEN CACCIATORE

6 to 8 breaded chicken tenders
12 ounces spaghetti
Prepared low-fat spaghetti sauce

Brown chicken tenders in a nonstick skillet; pat excess fat off with a paper towel. Cut into bite-size pieces. Set aside.

Prepare spaghetti according to package directions and drain.

Heat spaghetti sauce (I use Healthy Choice; it is very low in fat). Add chicken. Serve over spaghetti with salad and garlic toast.

Garlic Toast: To make garlic toast without a lot of fat, spray your bread with vegetable oil cooking spray and sprinkle with garlic salt or garlic powder. Brown in a nonstick skillet

SERVES 6

3 GRAMS FAT
EACH

Prep :10
Cook :50
Stand :00
Total 1:00

RUSSIAN CHICKEN

SERVES 6

4 GRAMS FAT

Prep :15
Cook :15
Stand :00
Total :30

6 to 8 boneless, skinless chicken breast halves
1 (8-ounce) bottle low-fat Russian salad dressing
1 envelope dry onion soup mix, such as Lipton's
1 (8-ounce) jar apricot preserves

Preheat the oven to 350 degrees. Spray a baking pan with vegetable oil cooking spray. Arrange the chicken pieces in the pan and spray them lightly. Bake uncovered, without turning, for 30 minutes. Drain off the pan juices.

Mix together the Russian dressing, soup mix, and apricot preserves. Pour over the drained cooked chicken and bake another 20 to 30 minutes, or until hot and bubbly.

HAWAIIAN STUFFED CHICKEN

SERVES 4

2 GRAMS FAT
EACH

Prep :20
Cook :40
Stand :00
Total 1:00

4 boneless, skinless chicken breast halves
²/₃ cup hot water
2 tablespoons Butter Buds
2 cups Stove Top stuffing, chicken flavor
1 medium green bell pepper, seeded and chopped
1 (8-ounce) can crushed pineapple, undrained
2 tablespoons brown sugar
2 tablespoons vinegar
¹/₄ teaspoon ground ginger

Preheat the oven to 400 degrees. Lay the chicken breasts on a flat surface and pound with a rolling pin or meat mallet to ¹/₄-inch thickness.

Mix the hot water and Butter Buds in a bowl. Stir in the stuffing mix, green pepper, and half the pineapple and juice.

Spoon the stuffing mix evenly over the chicken. Roll up tightly, starting with a long end. Secure with toothpicks. Place seam side down in a square baking dish that has been coated with vegetable oil cooking spray. Place any leftover stuffing in the middle.

Mix the remaining pineapple and juice with the brown sugar, vinegar, and ginger. Spoon over the chicken.

Bake uncovered, without turning, for 30 to 40 minutes, or until tender.

POLYNESIAN CHICKEN

2¹/₂ pounds meaty chicken pieces, skinned
1 (14-ounce) can crushed pineapple, undrained
1 small jar peach or apricot preserves

SERVES 4

Preheat the oven to 400 degrees. Spray a rectangular baking pan with vegetable oil cooking spray. Arrange the chicken pieces in the pan and spray them lightly. Bake uncovered for 30 minutes. Turn the chicken pieces and bake for an additional 15 or 20 minutes, or until tender. Drain off the pan juices.

Mix the pineapple with the peach preserves. Pour over the drained chicken and bake for another 15 to 20 minutes, or until hot and bubbly.

2 GRAMS FAT
EACH

Prep :10
Cook :60
Stand :00
Total 1:10

CHICKEN AND DUMPLINGS

SERVES 6

VERY LOW-FAT

Prep :15
Cook :35
Stand :00
Total :50

3 cups water
6 to 8 boneless, skinless chicken breast halves
¹/₂ cup egg substitute
1 cup skim milk   *omit - make*
2 cups self-rising flour   *bisquick   dumplings*

In a large saucepan, bring the water to a boil over high heat. Add the chicken pieces, return to a boil, and lower the heat. Cover and simmer until chicken is fork tender, 20 to 30 minutes.

Defat the stock. Return the chicken and stock to the saucepan and bring to a boil while you mix the dumplings.

In a medium bowl, mix the egg substitute and skim milk into the flour to form a soft dough. Drop by spoonfuls into the hot broth. Let boil 15 minutes without stirring. Do not cover.

Variations: Turn the dough out onto a floured board and roll to the desired thickness. Cut into squares and drop into the boiling broth; boil for 15 minutes. The broth may be thickened with 1 tablespoon cornstarch mixed in ¹/₄ cup of cold water or cold skim milk. Season to taste.

If you like a tougher type of dumpling, let the dough rest for ¹/₂ to 1 hour after you have rolled it out on a floured board. Cut into strips or squares and cook as directed above.

CREAMY CHICKEN AND NOODLES

2 cups water
4 boneless, skinless chicken breast halves
6 ounces cholesterol-free noodles
2 cups skim milk, or as needed
2 tablespoons cornstarch
2 cups cooked fresh vegetables (cut-up asparagus, corn kernels, green peas, etc.)

SERVES 4

2.05 GRAMS
FAT PER
SERVING

Prep :15
Cook :45
Stand :00
Total 1:00

Bring the water to a boil in a large saucepan over high heat. Add the chicken breasts, return to a boil, and lower the heat. Cover and simmer to desired degree of doneness, about 30 minutes. Remove from pan with a slotted spoon. Defat the stock; set chicken aside.

Return the stock to the pan and bring to a boil. Add the noodles and boil until tender but still firm, about 15 minutes. Drain in a colander (reserve stock for another purpose).

Return noodles to the pan, cover with 1 cup skim milk, and turn heat on to medium. While noodles are heating, mix 2 tablespoons of cornstarch with 1 cup cold milk. When noodles are hot, add the cornstarch mixture while stirring. Add the chicken and vegetables. Remove from the heat when the dish reaches the desired thickness.

Variation: Omit the cooked vegetables. Serve cut-up raw vegetables on the side.

CHICKEN NOODLE CASSEROLE

SERVES 6

2 GRAMS FAT

Prep :10
Cook 1:00
Stand :00
Total 1:10

6 to 8 breaded chicken tenders
2 cups cholesterol-free noodles
1 (8-ounce) can cream of mushroom soup, Healthy Request
1 (14-ounce) can fat-free chicken broth

Preheat the oven to 350 degrees. Brown the chicken on both sides in a dry nonstick skillet. Blot up any excess fat that has cooked out of the chicken.

Cook the noodles in a large pot of boiling salted water until tender, about 15 to 20 minutes. Drain. Coat a casserole dish with vegetable oil cooking spray. Add the noodles. Cut the chicken in bite-size pieces and place over the noodles.

Mix the soup and broth together with a whisk until smooth. Pour over the chicken and noodles. Bake about 45 minutes, until thick and creamy.

Chicken Rice Casserole: Rice may be substituted for noodles, if desired. Cook 1 cup regular or converted rice according to package directions and proceed with the recipe.

CHICKEN AND RIGATONI

6 to 8 breaded chicken tenders
$^1/_2$ cup chopped onion
$^1/_4$ cup chopped green pepper
$^1/_2$ pound rigatoni (about 2$^1/_2$ cups)
2 (10$^3/_4$-ounce) cans pasta-style tomatoes
1 (4-ounce) can V-8 juice
$^1/_2$ tomato can water
$^1/_2$ teaspoon basil
$^1/_2$ teaspoon oregano
Salt and pepper to taste

SERVES 6

4 GRAMS FAT

Prep :10
Cook :30
Stand :00
Total :40

Sauté the chicken tenders, onion, and green pepper in a large nonstick skillet that has been sprayed with vegetable oil cooking spray. Cook until lightly browned.

Meanwhile, cook the rigatoni according to package directions until just tender. Drain and keep warm.

When the chicken is done, blot off any fat that cooked out. Add the tomatoes, V-8 juice, water, and pasta. Stir in the seasonings and simmer until well blended.

BAKED CHICKEN REUBEN

SERVES 4

2 GRAMS FAT
PER SERVING

Prep :10
Cook 1:00
Stand :00
Total 1:10

4 boneless, skinless chicken breast halves
$1/4$ teaspoon salt
$1/8$ teaspoon pepper
2 cups sauerkraut, drained
$1 1/4$ cups low-calorie Russian salad dressing
4 slices fat-free Swiss cheese
1 tablespoon chopped parsley
Chopped chives

Preheat the oven to 325 degrees. Coat a small glass or ceramic baking dish with vegetable oil cooking spray.

Arrange the chicken pieces in the dish and sprinkle with salt and pepper. Cover the chicken with sauerkraut. Pour the dressing evenly over all and top with the cheese and parsley.

Cover with foil and bake 1 hour, or until fork tender. Sprinkle with chopped chives to serve.

CREOLE CHICKEN AND RICE

SERVES 4

VERY LOW-FAT

Prep :15
Cook :15
Stand :05
Total :35

$1/4$ teaspoon salt
$3/4$ cup instant rice, uncooked
4 boneless, skinless chicken breast halves
1 (8-ounce) can tomato sauce
$1/4$ cup chopped onion
2 tablespoons chopped green pepper
1 clove garlic, chopped fine
$1/2$ teaspoon dried basil
$1/8$ teaspoon pepper

Combine $3/4$ cup water and the salt in a small saucepan. Bring to a boil. Remove from the heat, stir in the rice, cover, and let stand 5 minutes. Keep warm while you make the chicken.

Coat a large nonstick skillet with vegetable oil cooking spray. Place over medium heat until hot. Add the chicken and cook until brown and tender, about 10 to 12 minutes, turning once. Add the tomato sauce, onion, green pepper, garlic, basil, pepper, and $\frac{1}{4}$ cup water. Bring to a boil, cover, reduce the heat, and simmer 6 minutes, stirring occasionally. Serve with the rice.

CANADIAN BACO CHICKO

6 to 8 breaded chicken tenders (or boneless, skinless chicken tenders)
$\frac{1}{2}$ cup chopped onion
$\frac{1}{2}$ cup chopped green pepper
$\frac{3}{4}$ cup shredded Canadian bacon
1 teaspoon minced garlic
2 (8-ounce) cans low-salt stewed tomatoes
$1\frac{1}{2}$ cups frozen green peas
$1\frac{1}{2}$ cups cholesterol-free noodles or macaroni
Salt and pepper to taste

SERVES 6

3 TO 4 GRAMS
FAT PER
SERVING

Prep :10
Cook :35
Stand :00
Total :45

Brown the chicken on both sides in a nonstick skillet. Add the onion, green pepper, Canadian bacon, and garlic. Sauté for 5 to 6 minutes, stirring to let onions, peppers, and bacon cook evenly.

Add the tomatoes and peas. Simmer for 10 to 12 minutes, stirring occasionally.

Meantime, cook noodles or macaroni (I use spiral macaroni) in a large pot of boiling water until nearly tender. Drain. Add to the chicken and sauce and continue to simmer about 10 more minutes. Correct seasoning.

WHITE CHICKEN CHILI

SERVES 8

2 GRAMS FAT
PER 1½-CUP
SERVING

Prep :20
Cook 1:30
Stand :00
Total 1:50

1 teaspoon lemon pepper
1 teaspoon cumin seed
4 boneless, skinless chicken breast halves
1 clove garlic, chopped fine
1 cup chopped onion
2 (8-ounce) cans white shoepeg corn, drained
2 (4-ounce) cans chopped green chiles, undrained
1 teaspoon ground cumin
2 to 3 tablespoons lime juice
2 (14-ounce) cans white or Great Northern beans, undrained
²/₃ cup crushed tortilla chips
²/₃ cup shredded fat-free Monterey jack cheese

In a large saucepan, combine 2½ cups of water with the lemon pepper and cumin seed. Bring to a boil. Add the chicken breast halves and return to a boil. Reduce the heat to low and simmer 20 to 30 minutes, or until the chicken is fork tender and the juices run clear.

Remove the chicken from the pan and cut into tiny pieces. Defat the broth, return to the saucepan, and place the chicken back in the stock.

Spray a medium skillet with vegetable oil cooking spray, add the garlic, and cook and stir over low heat 1 minute (careful not to burn garlic—it is terrible). Add to the chicken, then sauté the onions in the same skillet, cooking until tender. Add the cooked onions, corn, chiles, cumin, and lime juice to the chicken mixture. Bring to a boil.

Add beans and simmer until thoroughly heated, about 45 minutes. To serve, place about 1 tablespoon each of tortilla chips and cheese in 8 individual soup bowls, ladle hot chili over, and serve with salsa.

ZUCCHINI, CHICKEN, AND RICE

6 breaded chicken tenders
¹/₂ cup chopped onion
¹/₄ cup chopped green pepper
³/₄ cup chopped celery
1 cup chopped zucchini
1 (16-ounce) can stewed tomatoes
¹/₂ teaspoon minced garlic, or to taste
¹/₄ teaspoon crushed oregano leaves
¹/₄ teaspoon crushed basil leaves
¹/₄ teaspoon adobo seasoning
¹/₄ teaspoon Creole seasoning
3 cups hot cooked rice

SERVES 4

2 GRAMS FAT
PER SERVING

Prep :15
Cook :25
Stand :00
Total :40

Brown chicken on one side in a nonstick skillet. Add the onion, green pepper, and celery. Sauté for a short while, adding about ¹/₄ cup of water. Move the chicken around a little to move the flavor around.

Turn the chicken over and add the zucchini, tomatoes, and spices. Simmer for about 20 minutes, stirring a little now and then. As you stir, cut the chicken with a spatula into bite-size pieces. The breading on the chicken will thicken the sauce as you simmer and move it around.

When all is tender and thickened somewhat, serve on a bed of rice.

CHICKEN SALAD

SERVES 6

2 GRAMS FAT
(WITHOUT
PECANS)

Prep :30
Cook :20
Stand :00
Total :50

4 chicken breast halves, skinned
1 cup chopped celery
1 cup chopped sweet pickles
3 egg whites, boiled and chopped (discard the yolks—*bad!!*)
1 large apple, chopped
³/₄ cup pecans, chopped (optional)
Fat-free mayonnaise
Salt and pepper to taste

In a medium saucepan, bring 2½ cups of water to a boil. Add the chicken, return to a boil, and lower the heat. Simmer, covered, until the chicken is fork-tender and the juices run clear, 20 to 30 minutes. When the chicken is cool enough to handle, debone it and chop into small pieces. Reserve the broth in the refrigerator to defat and use later.

Combine chicken in a bowl with the remaining ingredients. Add enough mayonnaise to make as moist as you desire.

SEASONED RICE AND CHICKEN CASSEROLE

SERVES 4

3 GRAMS FAT

Prep :10
Cook :60
Stand :00
Total 1:10

1 (8-ounce) can condensed Special Request cream of mushroom soup, low-fat and low-sodium
1 cup skim milk
1 (8-ounce) can sliced water chestnuts, drained
1 (6-ounce) package long-grain and wild rice mix
1 (4-ounce) can mushroom stems and pieces, drained
1 (2-ounce) jar sliced pimientos, drained
3 cups cooked chicken or turkey, cubed

Preheat the oven to 350 degrees. In a mixing bowl, combine the soup, milk, and 1 cup of water. Stir with a whisk until smooth. Add all the remaining ingredients. Mix well.

Pour into an ungreased 3-quart casserole. Cover and bake for 30 minutes. Uncover, stir, and bake for an additional 30 to 45 minutes, or until rice is tender, stirring once again halfway through baking.

CHICKEN TORTILLA CASSEROLE

6 boneless, skinless chicken breast halves, cut into thin strips
1/2 cup sliced green onions
1 clove garlic, minced
3 tablespoons cornstarch
4 cups cold chicken broth, defatted
1 1/2 cups shredded fat-free Monterey jack cheese
1/2 cup fat-free salad dressing, such as Miracle Whip
1/2 cup fat-free sour cream
1 (4-ounce) can chopped green chiles, undrained
1/2 cup ripe olives
1/4 cup chopped parsley
12 (7-inch) flour tortillas

SERVES 6

VERY LOW-FAT

Prep :20
Cook :40
Stand :00
Total 1:00

Preheat the oven to 350 degrees.

Heat a nonstick skillet and spray with vegetable oil cooking spray. Add the chicken, onions, and garlic. Cook, stirring frequently, until the chicken is golden and cooked through, about 10 minutes. Remove the skillet from the heat and set aside.

In a saucepan stir together the cornstarch and cold chicken broth. Bring to a boil, stirring constantly. Boil 1 minute. Mix in 1 cup of the cheese, the salad dressing, sour cream, chiles, 1/4 cup of the olives, and parsley. Stir the sauce until smooth.

Remove 1 cup of sauce and stir into the chicken mixture. Spoon 2 tablespoons of the chicken mixture into each tortilla; roll to enclose. Place the tortillas seam side down in a 9 x 13-inch baking dish. Pour the remaining sauce over and top with the remaining cheese and olives. Bake for 25 minutes, or until thoroughly heated.

ALMOND CHICKEN CASSEROLE

SERVES 6

8 GRAMS FAT
ENTIRE DISH

Prep :15
Cook :35
Stand :00
Total :50

1 cup fresh bread cubes
1 tablespoon Butter Buds liquid
3 cups chopped cooked white-meat chicken
1½ cups chopped celery
1 cup fat-free salad dressing, such as Miracle Whip
1 cup shredded fat-free Swiss cheese
1 cup green bell pepper strips
¼ cup slivered almonds, toasted
¼ cup chopped onion

Preheat the oven to 350 degrees. Combine the bread cubes and Butter Buds; toss lightly. Set aside.

In a mixing bowl, combine the remaining ingredients; mix lightly. Spoon into a medium baking dish. Top with bread cubes. Bake uncovered for 30 to 35 minutes, or until lightly browned.

CHICKEN POTATO CASSEROLE

SERVES 6

2 GRAMS FAT

Prep :10
Cook :45
Stand :00
Total :55

This is a good Sunday morning quick casserole to leave cooking while in church. Just adjust the temperature of the oven down to about 300 degrees, depending on how long you will be gone. Do you have a short-winded preacher or does yours get his second wind around 12:00? If so, adjust down to about 250 degrees. You know your oven and your preacher!

6 to 8 breaded chicken tenders
3 to 4 potatoes, peeled and sliced thin
1 (10-ounce) package frozen green peas
2 (10¾-ounce) cans Healthy Request condensed cream of mushroom soup

Preheat the oven to 350 degrees. Brown the chicken on both sides in a nonstick skillet. Spray a medium-size casserole with vegetable oil cooking spray. Put the potatoes in the bottom of the casserole; add the peas for the second layer and the chicken for the third layer. (Blot any excess fat that cooked out of the chicken with paper towels before adding.)

Mix the cream of mushroom soup and 1 can of water with a wire whisk until smooth. Pour over casserole.

Bake about 45 minutes to 1 hour, or until golden and potatoes are tender.

MEXICAN CHICKEN CASSEROLE

1 large onion, chopped
3 medium tomatoes, peeled and chopped
2 cups chopped cooked white meat chicken
$^1/_2$ cup fat-free chicken broth
2 teaspoons chili powder
1 teaspoon salt
1 teaspoon ground cumin
1 teaspoon dried oregano
6 corn tortillas, cut into fourths
1 cup shredded fat-free Cheddar cheese

SERVES 6

2.09 GRAMS
FAT PER
SERVING

Prep :15
Cook :45
Stand :00
Total 1:00

Lightly spray an 11 x 7 x 1$^1/_2$-inch baking dish with vegetable oil cooking spray. Preheat the oven to 350 degrees.

Sauté the onion in $^1/_4$ cup water in a medium skillet until tender, stirring often. Add the tomato, chicken, broth, chili powder, salt, cumin, and oregano. Bring to a boil, reduce the heat, and simmer 5 to 6 minutes. Layer half the chicken mixture, half the tortillas, and half the cheese in the baking dish and repeat with the remaining chicken and tortillas. Reserve the remaining cheese. Cover the casserole and bake for 25 to 30 minutes.

Uncover and sprinkle evenly with the remaining $^1/_2$ cup cheese. Bake an additional 5 minutes, or until the cheese is bubbly.

Turkey

BAKED TURKEY AND DRESSING

SERVES 8

VERY LOW-FAT
DRESSING

Prep :30
Cook 3:00
Stand :00
Total 3:30

Turkey:
1 (8- to 12-pound turkey)
2 tablespoons flour

Dressing:
4 to 6 cups crumbled fat-free corn bread
2 cups chopped onions
1 stalk celery, chopped (2 cups)
2 to 4 tablespoons sage (or to taste; some like more)
1 cup defatted chicken broth
Salt and pepper to taste
$^3/_4$ cup egg substitute
Butter Buds or fat-free margarine

Preheat the oven to 350 degrees. Trim all visible fat off the neck and tail area of the turkey. Put 2 tablespoons of flour in a cooking bag and shake well. Place a rack or upside-down pie plate in a roaster pan. Place the turkey in the bag, punch holes in the bottom of the bag (this is to let the fat drain off), and punch holes in the top of the bag to let steam escape. Place the bagged turkey on the rack and bake for 2½ to 3 hours, or until a meat thermometer registers 180 degrees.

The dressing: Prepare the dressing so it can go into the oven in a separate baking dish for the last 45 minutes of cooking time. Spray a baking dish (make sure it will fit into the oven along with the turkey) with vegetable oil cooking spray.

Crumble the cold corn bread. Add the onions, celery, sage, broth, salt, pepper, and egg substitute. Mix well. Pour into the sprayed baking dish. Bake 30 minutes, or until about half done. Pour Butter Buds over the top or dot with fat-free margarine. Continue baking until desired doneness.

Variation: I simmer my celery and onions until tender and use part of the broth from them along with the chicken broth to moisten the dressing. Gives the dressing a very good flavor.

TURKEY OR CHICKEN GRAVY

2 to 2¹/₂ cups defatted chicken broth, or skim milk and water, mixed
¹/₄ cup poultry drippings, defatted as much as possible
¹/₄ cup flour
¹/₄ cup cold water
Salt and pepper to taste

SERVES 5

4 GRAMS FAT
PER ¹/₂-CUP
SERVING

Prep :05
Cook :10
Stand :00
Total :15

Heat the broth and add the hot liquid to the poultry drippings in the skillet or roasting pan. In a small bowl, combine the flour and cold water; mix until smooth. Add the flour mixture to the hot liquid while stirring with a whisk. Cook until mixture boils and thickens, stirring constantly. Season with salt and pepper.

TURKEY LO MEIN

SERVES 4

3 GRAMS FAT
PER 1¹/₃-CUP
SERVING

Prep :10
Cook :10
Stand :00
Total :20

2 cups cooked turkey breast strips
1 (14-ounce) can fat-free chicken broth
2 tablespoons light soy sauce
¹/₂ teaspoon sugar
¹/₂ to ³/₄ teaspoon ground ginger
¹/₄ teaspoon garlic powder
1 (16-ounce) package frozen broccoli, carrots, water chestnuts, and peppers
1 (4-ounce) package uncooked angel hair pasta or vermicelli
2 teaspoons cornstarch
2 tablespoons water

In a large skillet, combine the turkey, broth, soy sauce, sugar, ginger, garlic powder, and vegetables. Bring to a boil. Stir in the pasta. Reduce the heat to low, cover, and simmer 5 to 8 minutes, or until the pasta is tender.

In a small bowl combine the cornstarch and water; blend until smooth. Stir into the hot mixture in the skillet. Cook 1 minute, or until thickened, stirring constantly. Serve with additional soy sauce if desired.

TURKEY AND HAM À LA KING

A good recipe for that leftover holiday turkey and ham.

SERVES 8

6 GRAMS FAT

Prep :15
Cook :20
Stand :00
Total :35

¹/₄ cup chopped onion
2 tablespoons chopped green bell pepper
6 tablespoons flour
¹/₄ teaspoon white pepper
2 cups defatted chicken broth
1 cup skim milk
1¹/₂ cups diced cooked turkey or chicken
1¹/₂ cups diced lower-salt, 95% fat-free boneless ham
1 (2-ounce jar) sliced pimientos, drained
2 tablespoons sherry

Sauté the onion and green pepper in ¹/₄ cup water until tender. Stir in the flour and white pepper. Cook until smooth and bubbly. Gradually add the broth and milk. Cook until the mixture boils and thickens, stirring constantly. Boil 1 minute.

Stir in the turkey, ham, and pimientos; cook until thoroughly heated. Stir in the sherry just before serving.

Variation: Serve in patty shells if desired; this is also very good over rice.

TURKEY TAMALE PIE

SERVES 8

This is not only delicious—it's a pie that can be cooked on top of the stove and served right from the skillet.

VERY LOW-FAT

Prep :15
Cook :30
Stand :10
Total :55

¹/₂ cup yellow cornmeal
¹/₂ cup defatted chicken broth
¹/₃ cup no-fat plain yogurt
¹/₂ teaspoon salt
1 onion, chopped fine
1 clove garlic, chopped fine
8 ounces ground turkey
1 teaspoon chili powder
¹/₂ teaspoon crushed oregano leaves
¹/₂ teaspoon ground cumin
¹/₈ teaspoon pepper
1 (14-ounce) can stewed tomatoes, liquid and all
1 cup frozen whole-kernel corn
¹/₂ cup black olives, sliced
1 cup shredded fat-free Cheddar cheese

Combine the cornmeal, chicken broth, yogurt, and ¹/₄ teaspoon salt in a bowl. Set aside.

Sauté onion in ¹/₄ cup of water in a large skillet until tender. Add the garlic and cook 1 minute longer. Crumble the turkey into the skillet, sprinkle with chili powder, oregano, cumin, remaining ¹/₄ teaspoon salt, and pepper. Cook, stirring, until no pink remains. Blot with a paper towel to remove any excess fat.

Add the tomatoes and corn. Bring to a boil. Lower the heat to a simmer. Pour two-thirds of the cornmeal mixture into the simmering turkey mixture. Stir and simmer 3 minutes. (Do not let boil.)

Smooth the top with a spatula and scatter over ¹/₄ cup of the olives. Drizzle the remaining cornmeal mixture over the top.

Sprinkle with the cheese. Cover and simmer over very low heat, without stirring, for 15 to 20 minutes, or until set. Sprinkle with the remaining olives.

Remove from the heat. Let stand covered for 10 minutes. Serve hot, spooning onto plates.

TURKEY TORTILLA CASUAL

1 pound lean ground turkey
¹/₂ cup chopped onion
1 (8-ounce) jar Mexican salsa, green or red
¹/₂ cup fat-free sour cream
1 (10³/₄-ounce) can Healthy Request cream of chicken soup
1 (2-ounce) jar sliced pimientos, drained
6 corn tortillas, cut into 1-inch strips
2 cups shredded fat-free Cheddar cheese
Sliced olives (optional)

SERVES 4

LOW-FAT

Prep :15
Cook :45
Stand :10
Total 1:10

Preheat the oven to 350 degrees.

Cook and stir the ground turkey and onion in a nonstick skillet until brown. Transfer to a colander and rinse with hot water to wash away any excess fat. Shake dry.

Spread ¹/₂ cup of the salsa in the bottom of an ungreased square baking dish.

Mix the remaining salsa, the sour cream, soup, and pimientos. Layer half the tortilla strips, turkey mixture, soup mixture, and cheese in the baking dish. Repeat.

Bake uncovered until the casserole is hot and bubbly, about 30 minutes. Let stand 10 minutes. Garnish with olives if desired.

SANTA FE TURKEY TOSTADAS

SERVES 3

5 GRAMS FAT
EACH

Prep :15
Cook :25
Stand :00
Total :40

6 flour tortillas (8-inch)
1 pound ground turkey breast
1/2 cup chopped onion
1 (16-ounce) package frozen corn with red and green peppers
1 (14-ounce) can tomato sauce
3 to 4 teaspoons chili powder
1 1/2 teaspoons cumin
1/2 teaspoon garlic powder
3 cups shredded lettuce
1 large tomato, diced
1/2 cup shredded fat-free Cheddar cheese
Salsa if desired
Fat-free sour cream if desired

Heat the oven to 375 degrees. Place the tortillas on an ungreased cookie sheet. Bake for 7 to 10 minutes, or until crisp and lightly browned.

Meanwhile, spray a large nonstick skillet with vegetable oil cooking spray. Brown the turkey with the onion; drain well. Pat out any excess fat or rinse in a colander under hot water.

Return the turkey to the pan. Add the corn, tomato sauce, chili powder, cumin, and garlic powder. Bring to a boil, reduce the heat, and simmer 6 to 8 minutes, stirring occasionally.

To assemble: Place baked tortillas on individual serving plates, top with 1/6 of lettuce, spoon 1/6 of meat mixture over lettuce. Top each with tomato and cheese. Serve with salsa and a dollop of fat-free sour cream.

Meat and Fish

SWISS STEAK

SERVES 4

4 GRAMS FAT
PER SERVING

Prep :15
Cook 1:30
Stand :00
Total 1:45

1 pound lean boneless sirloin steak, trimmed of all fat
1 cup tomato juice or stewed tomatoes
1 large onion, sliced thin and separated into rings
1 large green bell pepper, sliced into thin rounds
Salt and pepper to taste

Spray a nonstick skillet with vegetable oil cooking spray. Brown the steak well on both sides. Pour off or blot away any fat. Return the meat to the skillet and add the remaining ingredients. Cover and simmer about 1¼ hours, or to desired doneness.

Note: The meat may be transferred to a covered baking dish and cooked in a 350 degree oven until tender if so desired.

MEXICALI PORK CHOP CASSEROLE

SERVES 4

8 GRAMS FAT
PER SERVING

Prep :15
Cook :27
Stand :00
Total :42

Studies say that pork chops (butterfly and center-cut) are equal to chicken in fat content if trimmed of all fat. You be the judge. I'm very careful and seldom serve pork, but it is nice for a change, and won't hurt you if you serve it in moderation.

1 large onion, halved and sliced thin
½ medium green bell pepper, chopped
½ medium red bell pepper, chopped
1 (12-ounce) can low-sodium stewed tomatoes, drained and chopped
1 cup frozen whole-kernel corn, thawed and drained
¼ teaspoon dried marjoram
4 lean pork chops, trimmed of all fat

Preheat the oven to 350 degrees. Spray a nonstick skillet with vegetable oil cooking spray.

Sauté the onion and peppers in the skillet for about 5 minutes. Add the tomatoes, corn, and marjoram, raise the heat, and cook uncovered 5 minutes longer. Pour into 1½-quart casserole coated with cooking spray.

In the same skillet brown the chops for 2 minutes on each side. Lay the chops on top of the vegetable mixture.

Cover the casserole and bake 12 to 15 minutes, or until the chops are done.

HAM, NOODLE, AND GREEN PEA CASSEROLE

6 ounces cholesterol-free noodles
1½ tablespoons flour
1 teaspoon dry mustard
¼ teaspoon ground sage
⅛ teaspoon grated nutmeg
⅛ teaspoon pepper
1½ cups skim milk
6 ounces 98% fat-free ham, cubed
2 cups frozen green peas
2 tablespoons Butter Buds liquid
2 tablespoons bread crumbs, fat-free bread (1 slice)

SERVES 4

3 GRAMS FAT

Prep :10
Cook :30
Stand :00
Total :40

Preheat the oven to 350 degrees.

Cook the noodles according to package directions, but leave out the salt. Drain well and set aside.

In a saucepan or skillet, combine the flour, mustard, sage, nutmeg, and pepper. Slowly whisk in the milk and set aside.

In a mixing bowl, combine the noodles, ham, and frozen peas. Pour the milk mixture over and mix well. Transfer to a shallow baking dish. Pour the Butter Buds over.

Cover with foil. Bake 10 to 15 minutes. Uncover, sprinkle with the bread crumbs, and bake 10 to 15 minutes longer.

BREAKFAST SAUSAGE CASSEROLE

SERVES 8

VERY LOW-FAT

Prep :20
Cook :30
Stand 8:00
Total 8:50

1 (4-ounce) can chopped green chiles
1½ cups shredded fat-free Cheddar cheese
1 pound low-fat sausage, cooked, crumbled, rinsed with hot water, and drained
2 cups egg substitute
1 cup skim milk

Line the bottom of an 8-inch square baking dish with half the green chiles. Add half the cheese, then the remaining chiles, then all the sausage. Top with the remaining cheese. Refrigerate overnight.

The next morning, preheat the oven to 400 degrees. Beat together the egg substitute and milk. Pour over the casserole and bake uncovered for 30 minutes.

BREAKFAST SAUSAGE BAKE

SERVES 8

3 GRAMS FAT
PER SERVING

Prep :15
Cook :45
Stand :00
Total 1:00

1 pound fresh mushrooms, chopped fine
1 cup fine dry bread crumbs
1 pound low-fat sausage (3 grams fat per patty) or turkey breakfast sausages
1 green or red bell pepper, cored and chopped
1 tablespoon dried parsley flakes
¼ teaspoon cayenne pepper
2 (8-ounce) cartons egg substitute

Preheat the oven to 350 degrees.

Heat ¼ cup of water in a nonstick skillet and add the mushrooms. Cook and stir until the mixture boils and the moisture evaporates. Remove from the heat. Stir in the bread crumbs.

Spray a 9 x 13 x 2-inch baking dish with vegetable oil cooking spray. Press the mushroom mixture onto the bottom of the prepared baking dish to form crust.

In the same nonstick skillet cook the sausage, breaking apart or crumbling into small pieces and stirring frequently until lightly browned. Remove from the heat. Put into a colander and rinse with hot water; shake well.

In a mixing bowl, combine the sausage, chopped pepper, parsley, and cayenne. Spread the sausage mixture over crust. Pour the egg substitute evenly over the sausage. Bake uncovered 25 to 30 minutes, or until the mixture is set.

SAUSAGE SCALLOPED POTATOES

1 pound turkey sausages
1 (10³/₄-ounce) can Healthy Request cream of mushroom soup
³/₄ cup skim milk
¹/₂ cup chopped onion
¹/₂ teaspoon salt
¹/₄ teaspoon pepper
3 cups thinly sliced potatoes
Butter Buds
¹/₂ pound shredded fat-free Cheddar cheese

SERVES 8

VERY LOW-FAT

Prep :20
Cook 2:00
Stand :00
Total 2:20

Preheat the oven to 350 degrees. Cook the sausages in a non-stick skillet, breaking apart and stirring frequently until lightly browned. Transfer to a colander and run hot water over to wash away any excess fat. Drain well.

In a mixing bowl, combine the soup, milk, onion, salt, and pepper. In a large casserole sprayed with vegetable oil cooking spray, layer half the potatoes, half the soup mixture, and half the sausage. Repeat the layers, ending with sausage.

Stream Butter Buds over the top lightly. Bake for 1¹/₂ hours or until potatoes are tender. Sprinkle with cheese, and return to the oven for another 15 minutes.

SAUSAGE AND NOODLE CASSEROLE

SERVES 6

VERY LOW-FAT

Prep :20
Cook :45
Stand :00
Total 1:05

1 pound turkey sausages
$^1\!/_2$ cup chopped onion
$^1\!/_4$ cup chopped green pepper
1 (10$^3\!/_4$-ounce) can Healthy Request cream of chicken soup
1 (8-ounce package) noodles (no yolk, no cholesterol, fat-free), cooked and
    drained
Salt and pepper to taste

Preheat the oven to 350 degrees.

Crumble the sausage in a large nonstick skillet; add the onion and green pepper. Cook, stirring, over medium heat until the meat is browned and vegetables are tender. Drain and rinse under hot water in a colander; shake off excess water.

Combine soup with 1$^1\!/_3$ cups of water in a large bowl. Stir until smooth. Add the meat mixture, noodles, salt, and pepper. Mix well. Spoon into a 9 x 11-inch baking dish. Bake uncovered for 30 minutes, or until bubbly.

SAUSAGE AND RICE CASSEROLE

SERVES 6

VERY LOW-FAT

Prep :15
Cook 1:30
Stand :00
Total 1:45

1 pound turkey sausages
1 green bell pepper, seeded and chopped
1 onion, chopped
4 stalks celery, chopped
1 (10$^3\!/_4$-ounce) can Healthy Request cream of chicken soup
1 cup brown rice
3 tablespoons slivered almonds

Preheat the oven to 350 degrees. Heat a large nonstick skillet and cook the sausage, breaking apart and stirring frequently, until it begins to brown. Add the pepper, onion, and celery and continue cooking until the vegetables are tender. Transfer to a colander and rinse under hot water; shake dry.

Combine the soup in a saucepan with enough water to measure

4 cups. Add the turkey and vegetables, bring to a boil, and simmer 5 minutes. Add the raw rice and almonds. Pour into a 9 x 13 x 2-inch baking dish, cover, and bake for 1 hour.

SPAGHETTI PIE

6 ounces spaghetti
3 tablespoons Butter Buds
$^1/_2$ tablespoon egg substitute
$^1/_2$ cup grated fat-free Parmesan cheese
1 pound turkey sausages
$^1/_2$ cup chopped onion
$^1/_4$ cup chopped green pepper
1 (8-ounce) can tomatoes, cut up, with their juice
1 (6-ounce) can tomato paste
1 teaspoon sugar
1 teaspoon oregano
$^1/_4$ teaspoon garlic salt
1 cup fat-free cottage cheese, drained
$^1/_2$ cup shredded fat-free mozzarella cheese

SERVES
4 TO 6

8 GRAMS FAT

Prep :15
Cook 1:00
Stand :00
Total 1:15

Preheat the oven to 350 degrees.

In a saucepan, cook the spaghetti according to package directions; drain and return to the pan. Stir in the Butter Buds, egg substitute, and Parmesan cheese. Press the spaghetti into a pie plate that has been sprayed with vegetable oil cooking spray, forming a crust.

In a nonstick skillet, cook the turkey sausage with the onion and green pepper, stirring to break apart the sausage, until brown. Drain, place in a colander, and rinse with hot water to remove any excess fat. Place in a saucepan; stir in the tomatoes, tomato paste, sugar, oregano, and garlic salt. Heat thoroughly. Spread cottage cheese over the bottom of the spaghetti crust. Top with the meat mixture.

Bake uncovered for 20 minutes. Sprinkle with mozzarella and bake 5 minutes more, or until the cheese is melted.

HAM AND POTATOES AU GRATIN

SERVES 4

VERY LOW-FAT

Prep :10
Cook :45
Stand :00
Total :45

1 pound frozen hash brown potatoes (check label for fat content)
1¹/₂ cups cubed 98% fat-free ham
1 cup shredded fat-free Cheddar cheese
¹/₂ cup fat-free salad dressing, such as Miracle Whip
¹/₂ cup skim milk
¹/₂ cup dry bread crumbs
1 tablespoon Butter Buds, liquid form
Salt and pepper to taste

Preheat the oven to 350 degrees.

Combine the potatoes, ham, and cheese; mix lightly. Combine the salad dressing and milk; mix well. Add the dressing mixture to the potato mixture and mix lightly. Spoon into a 1-quart casserole.

Combine the bread crumbs and Butter Buds. Sprinkle over the potato mixture. Bake uncovered for 40 to 50 minutes, or until thoroughly heated.

BREAKFAST HAM CASSEROLE

SERVES 4

4 GRAMS FAT
PER 1-CUP
SERVING

Prep :10
Cook :30
Stand 8:30
Total 9:10

3 cups cubed French bread
³/₄ cup diced 98% fat-free ham
2 tablespoons diced sweet red bell pepper
1 cup shredded fat-free Cheddar cheese
1¹/₃ cups skim milk
³/₄ cup egg substitute
¹/₄ teaspoon dry mustard
¹/₄ teaspoon onion powder
¹/₄ teaspoon white pepper
Paprika

Arrange bread cubes evenly in an 8-inch square baking dish. Layer the ham, red bell pepper, and cheese over the bread. Set aside.

Combine the milk, egg substitute, mustard, onion powder, and white pepper. Pour over the cheese. Cover and refrigerate at least 8 hours. Remove from the refrigerator and let stand 30 minutes. Meantime, heat the oven to 350 degrees.

Bake the casserole uncovered for 30 minutes, or until puffy and golden. Sprinkle with paprika. Serve immediately.

Variation: One pound of turkey sausage, cooked, drained, and crumbled, may be substituted for the ham. (Pat out any and all excess fat with a paper towel, or place the browned meat in a colander and rinse with hot water.) Twelve grams of fat per serving.

IN FISH, FAT IS NOT A DIRTY WORD

A lean high-quality protein source, fish contains three fatty acids that are thought to help lower blood cholesterol.

Low-Fat Fish (Less Than 5%)

Catfish	Halibut
Black sea bass	Monkfish
Cod	Orange roughy
Flounder	Pollock
Grouper	Red snapper
Haddock	Rockfish
Sole	Sea trout
Striped bass	Swordfish
Whiting	Tilapia
Perch	

Moderately Fat Fish (5–10%)

Bluefish	Trout
Butterfish	Tuna
Carp	Whitefish

Higher Fat Fish (Over 10%)

Herring	Salmon
Mackerel	Sardine
Pompano	

Source: USDA Handbook 8

BAKED "FRIED" CATFISH

Catfish fillets   *pepper*
Egg substitute   *Garlic powder*
Cornflake crumbs

2 GRAMS FAT

Prep :10
Cook :25
Stand :00
Total :35

Preheat the oven to 400 degrees.

Spray a heavy metal baking sheet or pan with vegetable oil cooking spray.

Dip the fillets in the egg substitute. Roll in cornflake crumbs. Place on the baking sheet and spray the fillets lightly with cooking spray.

Bake about 25 minutes, or until crisp and flaky. Turn over when half done to brown and crisp both sides nicely.

Serve w/ lowfat Tartar sauce

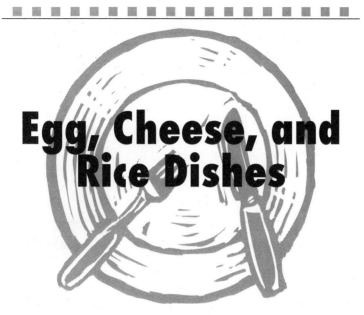

Egg, Cheese, and Rice Dishes

EASY GARDEN QUICHE

SERVES 2

6 GRAMS FAT

Prep :10
Cook :40
Stand :05
Total :55

2 cups chopped fresh broccoli
$^1/_2$ cup chopped onion
$^1/_2$ cup chopped green bell pepper
1 cup shredded fat-free Cheddar cheese
1$^1/_2$ cups skim milk
$^3/_4$ cup low-fat biscuit mix, such as Bisquick
1 teaspoon salt
$^1/_4$ teaspoon pepper
$^3/_4$ cup egg substitute

Heat the oven to 400 degrees. Lightly spray a pie plate with vegetable oil cooking spray. In a saucepan, heat 1 cup water with $^1/_2$ teaspoon salt to boiling. Add the broccoli and cook until tender; drain thoroughly.

Toss together the broccoli, onion, green pepper, and cheese and turn into the prepared pie plate. Beat the remaining ingredients until smooth (about 15 seconds in a blender). Pour over the veggies in the pie plate. Bake 35 to 40 minutes, or until golden brown and a knife inserted halfway between the center and the edge comes out clean. Let stand 5 minutes before cutting.

Variation: 1 package (10-ounce) frozen chopped broccoli or cauliflower, thawed and drained, can be substituted for fresh broccoli. Do not cook.

FIESTA QUICHE

4 flour tortillas
$^1/_2$ cup shredded fat-free Cheddar cheese
1 (4-ounce) can green chiles, drained and chopped
$^1/_4$ cup sliced green onions
$^1/_2$ cup picante sauce
1 cup egg substitute
$^1/_3$ cup skim milk
1 teaspoon chili powder
1 teaspoon pepper
Tomato wedges
Fat-free yogurt or sour cream
Cilantro

SERVES 2

2.5 GRAMS
PER SERVING

Prep :10
Cook :35
Stand :05
Total :50

Preheat the oven to 350 degrees. Spray a 12-inch quiche dish with vegetable oil cooking spray. Arrange the tortillas in dish. Sprinkle the cheese, chiles, and green onions over the tortillas. Dollop with picante sauce.

Combine the egg substitute, milk, chili powder, and pepper. Pour into the quiche dish.

Bake uncovered for 30 to 35 minutes. Remove from the oven. Arrange tomato wedges around the edge; top with a dot of fat-free yogurt or sour cream and a sprig of cilantro. Let stand 5 minutes before cutting into wedges to serve.

RICE AND TURKEY QUICHE

Good for leftover turkey from the holidays.

SERVES 4

6 GRAMS FAT
ENTIRE DISH

Prep :10
Cook :20
Stand :05
Total :35

3 cups cooked rice, cooled - *Brown*
1½ cups chopped cooked turkey - *Veg. crumbles - cooked*
1 medium tomato, seeded and chopped
¼ cup sliced green onions
¼ cup chopped green bell pepper
1 teaspoon dried basil
½ teaspoon seasoned salt
⅛ teaspoon cayenne pepper
½ cup skim milk
¾ cup egg substitute
1 cup shredded fat-free Cheddar cheese

Preheat the oven to 375 degrees. In a mixing bowl, combine the rice, turkey, tomato, onion, green pepper, basil, seasoned salt, cayenne, milk, and egg substitute. Pour into a square baking dish that has been coated with vegetable oil cooking spray. Top with the cheese.

Bake for 20 minutes, or until a knife inserted halfway between the edge and the center comes out clean. Let stand 5 minutes before serving.

ITALIAN OMELET

1 cup egg substitute
¹/₄ teaspoon salt
¹/₄ teaspoon Italian seasoning
¹/₈ teaspoon pepper
¹/₂ cup chopped onion
2 tablespoons chopped green pepper
1 clove garlic, chopped fine
³/₄ pound potatoes (about 4 small), peeled and cut into small dice
1 tablespoon fat-free Parmesan cheese
Salsa (optional)

SERVES 2

LESS THAN 1
GRAM FAT PER
SERVING

Prep :10
Cook :20
Stand :00
Total :30

Combine the egg substitute, salt, Italian seasoning, and pepper and set aside.

Heat 2 tablespoons of water in a skillet; add the onion, pepper, and garlic. Sauté until crisp tender. Add the potatoes and cook 5 to 8 minutes, stirring often, until they begin to brown. Spray lightly with vegetable oil cooking spray a couple of times to help brown.

Reduce the heat. Pour the egg substitute mixture over the vegetables in the skillet and sprinkle with Parmesan cheese. Cover and cook 7 to 8 minutes, or until set. Invert onto a plate and serve with salsa, if desired.

POCKET BREAKFAST

SERVES 4

0 GRAMS
FAT

Prep :10
Cook :10
Stand :00
Total :20

1 (8-ounce) carton egg substitute
³/₄ cup frozen or canned corn with red and green peppers
1 tablespoon chopped cilantro
Salt and pepper
¹/₄ cup shredded fat-free Cheddar cheese
2 whole wheat fat-free pocket (pita) breads, halved

Combine the egg substitute, vegetables, cilantro, and salt and pepper to taste. Mix well.

Spray a nonstick skillet with vegetable oil cooking spray. Add the egg mixture and cook until firm but moist, stirring occasionally. Sprinkle with the cheese. Spoon into pocket bread halves.

MOCK TAMALE PIE

SERVES 6

1 GRAM FAT
PER TAMALE

Prep :20
Cook :20
Stand :00
Total :40

1 package 6-inch corn tortillas (12 tortillas)
1 (14-ounce) can fat-free refried beans
2¹/₂ cups shredded fat-free Cheddar cheese
1 medium onion, chopped
2 cups fat-free vegetable chili—use leftovers from recipe on page 130 (see Note)
(Trader Joe's 3 Bean chili)

Preheat the oven to 350 degrees.

Warm the tortillas by dipping one at a time in hot water. Pat dry. Place 2 to 3 tablespoons of refried beans down the center of each. Top the beans with 2 tablespoons of shredded cheese and 1 teaspoon of onion.

Fold the tortillas around the filling and place seam side down in a 9 x 13 x 2-inch baking dish that has been sprayed with vegetable oil cooking spray. Pour the chili over the top and sprinkle with the remaining cheese.

Bake for about 20 minutes, or until the cheese inside the tortillas is melted. Serve with salad and baked flour tortilla chips.

Note: There is a fat-free canned chili available at the market that will work very nicely if no leftover chili is on hand.

BAKED CHEESE GRITS

4 cups skim milk
1¹/₂ cups quick-cooking hominy grits
1 cup shredded nonfat Cheddar cheese (4 ounces)
¹/₃ cup Butter Buds liquid
³/₄ cup egg substitute, slightly beaten
¹/₂ teaspoon salt
¹/₂ teaspoon crushed red pepper

SERVES 8

LESS THAN 1 GRAM FAT

Prep :15
Cook :45
Stand :00
Total 1:00

Heat the oven to 350 degrees. Spray a shallow 2¹/₂-quart baking dish, or eight 1¹/₂-cup individual baking dishes, with vegetable oil cooking spray.

Bring the milk and 2 cups of water to a boil in a large heavy saucepan. Watch carefully or it will boil over. Slowly stir in the grits. Stir until boiling, reduce the heat to low, and cook 4 to 6 minutes, stirring often, until thick.

Remove from the heat, stir in the cheese, then add the remaining ingredients. Stir until well blended and smooth.

Pour into the prepared dish or dishes. Bake until puffed and lightly browned, 25 to 30 minutes for individual dishes, 35 to 45 minutes for large baking dish.

BREAKFAST ON THE RUN

SERVES 1

VERY LOW-FAT

Prep :03
Cook :01
Stand :00
Total :04

1 slice fat-free bread
2 to 3 tablespoons fat-free cream cheese
1 banana
Cinnamon

Toast the bread, spread cream cheese over, slice the banana over the top, and sprinkle with cinnamon.

MEXICAN RICE

**SERVES
2 TO 3**

1 GRAM FAT

Prep :10
Cook :20
Stand :00
Total :35

¹/₂ cup chopped onion
¹/₂ cup chopped green bell pepper
2 cloves garlic, chopped fine
2 tablespoons Butter Buds liquid
1 cup rice
1 tomato, peeled, seeded, and chopped
2 cups defatted chicken broth
1 teaspoon cumin seeds

Sauté the onion, peppers, and garlic in 2 to 4 tablespoons of water until crisp but tender. Add the Butter Buds and rice; cook until the onions are soft but not brown. Stir in the tomatoes and cook 30 seconds more; add the broth and cumin. Bring to a boil; stir once or twice. Reduce the heat, cover, and simmer 15 minutes, or until the rice is tender.

RED BEANS AND RICE

1 package Cajun red beans, spices reserved (I shake about half the pepper off before using; it's too hot for Okies!)
Defatted ham stock or water
1 cup chopped celery
1 cup chopped onions
³/₄ cup chopped green pepper
Pepper and salt to taste
Hot cooked rice

SERVES 4

0 GRAMS FAT

Prep :10
Cook 4:00
Stand :00
Total 4:10

Boil the beans in ham stock to cover until tender, about 3 to 3¹/₂ hours. Meanwhile, sauté the celery, onions, and green pepper in ¹/₄ cup of water for 3 to 5 minutes.

When the beans are almost done, add the vegetables and simmer. Add 2 tablespoons of the Cajun seasoning (careful, just add a little at a time, it gets hot quick). Pepper and salt to taste. Simmer until very thick. Serve over rice.

CORN AND RICE CASSEROLE

1 green bell pepper, seeded and chopped
1 large onion, chopped
1¹/₂ cups rice
2 (14-ounce) cans cream-style corn
1 small jar pimientos, drained and chopped
¹/₄ cup egg substitute
2 tablespoons sugar
¹/₂ cup Butter Buds

SERVES 4

1 GRAM FAT

Prep :20
Cook :45
Stand :00
Total 1:05

Preheat the oven to 350 degrees.

Sauté the pepper and onion for 3 minutes in ¹/₄ cup water. Cook the rice according to package directions (leave out the butter).

Combine the pepper and onion, rice, and corn with the pimientos, egg substitute, sugar, and Butter Buds. Pour into a baking dish that has been sprayed with vegetable oil cooking spray. Spray the top lightly and bake uncovered for 25 to 30 minutes.

QUICK SPANISH RICE

SERVES 6

0 GRAMS FAT

Prep :10
Cook :20
Stand :00
Total :30

1 cup finely chopped onion
1 cup chopped celery
1 cup chopped green bell pepper
1 (8-ounce) can tomato sauce
1 (8-ounce) can tomatoes with their juice
1¹/₄ cups low-fat reduced-sodium chicken broth
1 teaspoon prepared mustard
1 bay leaf
¹/₂ teaspoon oregano
2 cups instant rice

In a saucepan, combine the onion, celery, green pepper, tomato sauce, tomatoes, broth, mustard, bay leaf, and oregano. Simmer for 10 to 12 minutes. Stir in the rice and simmer, covered, over very low heat for 5 to 6 minutes, stirring occasionally.

PINEAPPLE RICE

This is very good with grilled chicken.

SERVES 4

0 GRAMS FAT

Prep :10
Cook :05
Stand :00
Total :15

1 can pineapple tidbits in juice, undrained
1¹/₂ cups instant rice
¹/₄ teaspoon salt (optional)
¹/₄ teaspoon grated nutmeg
¹/₄ cup chopped fresh parsley

In a saucepan, combine the pineapple, rice, salt, nutmeg, and ¹/₂ cup water. Bring to a boil, reduce the heat, cover, and simmer about 5 minutes, or until rice is tender. Stir in the parsley.

RICE SALAD

1 cup cold cooked rice
1 (8-ounce) can kidney beans, drained and rinsed
1 tomato, peeled, seeded, and chopped
$^1/_2$ cup frozen whole-kernel corn (see Note)
1 tablespoon chopped green onion
2 tablespoons red wine vinegar
2 teaspoons canola oil
1 teaspoon dried basil
Salt and pepper to taste
Fresh spinach leaves (optional)

SERVES 2

**2 GRAMS FAT
PER SERVING**

**Prep :10
Cook :00
Stand :00
Total :10**

In a serving bowl, combine the rice, beans, tomato, corn, and chopped onion.

Whisk together the vinegar, oil, basil, salt, and pepper. Pour the dressing over the salad and toss lightly to mix. Serve on spinach leaves if desired.

Note: To quick-thaw the corn, run hot water over it while in a strainer.

Pasta and Pizza

Pasta

STUFFED MANICOTTI

1 (8-ounce) box manicotti shells
1 (16-ounce) carton ricotta cheese, soft
Dab of nutmeg
1 (10-ounce) package frozen spinach, cooked, squeezed dry, and chopped
Spaghetti sauce (Healthy Choice is good and low in fat)

SERVES 4

2 GRAMS FAT

Preheat the oven to 350 degrees. Spray a rectangular baking dish with vegetable oil cooking spray.

Cook and drain the pasta shells according to package directions. Set aside.

Mix the ricotta, nutmeg, and spinach. Stuff shells with the mixture. Arrange in the baking dish. Pour spaghetti sauce over and bake uncovered for 25 minutes, or until hot and bubbly.

Prep :20
Cook :40
Stand :00
Total 1:00

SPAGHETTI SAUCE

1 large onion, chopped
1 medium green bell pepper, seeded and chopped
2 cloves garlic, chopped fine
1 (14-ounce) can Italian tomatoes with their juice
1 (8-ounce) can sliced mushrooms (optional)
1 (8-ounce) can tomato sauce
Pinch of oregano
Pinch of basil
Dash of salt and pepper
2 tablespoons cornstarch

SERVES 2

0 GRAMS FAT

Prep :10
Cook :30
Stand :00
Total :40

In a large skillet, sauté the onion, green pepper, and garlic in ¼ cup of water for 3 to 5 minutes, or until crisp-tender. Add the tomatoes, mushrooms if using, tomato sauce, oregano, basil, salt, and pepper. Simmer for 20 to 30 minutes.

To thicken, mix the cornstarch with ¼ cup cold water; gradually stir into sauce, and cook 3 minutes longer.

VEGETARIAN LASAGNE

SERVES 6

LESS THAN 1
GRAM FAT
ENTIRE DISH

Prep :30
Cook 1:25
Stand :10
Total 2:05

1 medium onion, chopped
1 medium green pepper, seeded and chopped
1 (16-ounce) can tomatoes, undrained
1 (16-ounce) can kidney beans, drained and rinsed
3 tablespoons tomato paste
Dash of salt and pepper
1 teaspoon sugar
2 medium zucchini, chopped
1½ packages (about 18) no-boil lasagne noodles
16 ounces fat-free mozzarella cheese, shredded (2 cups)

Sauté the onion and pepper in ¼ cup water in a large nonstick skillet until tender.

Add the tomatoes, liquid, and all the beans, tomato paste, salt, pepper, sugar, and 2½ cups water. Heat to a boil. Reduce heat and simmer 15 minutes. Stir occasionally.

Sauté the zucchini in ¼ cup water in a separate pan until crisp-tender, about 5 minutes. Drain well.

Preheat the oven to 350 degrees. Spoon a third of the sauce evenly over the bottom of a 9 x 13 x 2-inch baking dish. Arrange half the noodles in a single layer overlapping to fit. Top with the zucchini, 3 cups of the cheese, and half the remaining sauce.

Next, layer on the rest of the noodles, the remaining sauce, and the remaining 1 cup of cheese.

Cover and bake 40 to 50 minutes. Uncover and bake 15 minutes longer. Let stand 10 minutes before cutting and serving.

LASAGNE WITH BEAN SAUCE

Sauce:
1 onion, chopped fine
2 teaspoons garlic, chopped fine
2 cups cooked beans (red or brown, canned or home cooked), drained and
    coarsely chopped
4 cups tomato purée, or 2 cups tomato sauce plus 2 cups purée
1 teaspoon oregano
1 teaspoon dried basil
Pepper to taste

³/₄ pound uncooked lasagne noodles
2 cups skim milk or fat-free ricotta cheese
8 ounces fat-free mozzarella cheese, sliced thin
¹/₄ cup grated fat-free Parmesan cheese

SERVES 6

.33 GRAMS FAT
PER SERVING

Prep :30
Cook 1:30
Stand :10
Total 2:10

Prepare the sauce: Sauté the onion in 2 tablespoons of water for a minute. Add garlic the last 10 seconds (be careful not to burn garlic—it's terrible!). Add the chopped beans. Cook this mixture, stirring, for several minutes longer. Add the tomato purée, oregano, basil, and pepper. Bring the sauce to a boil and simmer for 5 minutes. Meantime, heat the oven to 350 degrees.

To assemble the lasagne: Spread a thin layer of bean sauce on the bottom of a 9 x 13 x 2-inch baking dish. Arrange a layer of noodles to cover the bottom of the dish so they are touching but do not overlap. You should use about one third of the noodles. Cover the noodle layer with half the ricotta, half the mozzarella, and one third of the remaining sauce. Repeat with a layer of noodles, the remaining ricotta and mozzarella, and another third of the sauce.

Finish off with layers of remaining noodles and sauce. Sprinkle the Parmesan on top.

Cover the pan tightly with foil. Bake lasagne in the preheated oven for about 1 hour, or until the pasta is cooked. If there is too much liquid remaining in pan, remove the foil and bake for another 10 to 15 minutes. Let stand 10 minutes before serving.

Pizza

PIZZA CRUST

Have fun seeing how low-fat you can make your pizza, and how good. Your friends will not believe you when you tell them how low in fat it is. Use 98% fat-free ham or Canadian bacon, shredded, along with your vegetables and cheeses.

MAKES
TWO 12-
INCH
CRUSTS

1.05 GRAMS
FAT PER
SERVING

Prep :25
Cook :15
Stand 1:30
Total 2:10

1 package active dry yeast
1¹/₂ cups warm (not hot) water
1 teaspoon salt
2 tablespoons canola oil
4¹/₂ cups all-purpose flour, approximately

In a large bowl, sprinkle the yeast over the warm water and allow to soften for 5 to 10 minutes. Add the salt and oil and 3 cups of the flour; mix well. Add more flour, ¹/₂ cup at a time, beating with a wooden spoon, until you have a soft dough that is no longer sticky.

Turn the dough into a bowl sprayed with vegetable oil cooking spray; spray the top lightly. Cover with a kitchen towel damp with warm water and allow to rise for 1 to 1¹/₂ hours, or until doubled in bulk.

Punch the dough down, divide in half, and allow to rest for 15 minutes. Roll out on a floured surface as thick or thin as desired.

To prebake, place the rolled-out dough on a cookie sheet sprayed with cooking spray. Bake in a 450 degree oven for 15 to 20 minutes, until golden.

Note: Remember to stay in the fat-free cheeses and toppings. If you are in a hurry you can use Healthy Choice spaghetti sauce.

VEGGIE PIZZA

1 recipe Pizza Crust (page 114), unbaked

Pizza Sauce:
1/2 cup chopped green pepper
1 1/2 cups tomato sauce
2 tablespoons chopped garlic
1 teaspoon sugar
Pinch of salt
1 teaspoon oregano
2 teaspoons dried basil

Pizza Toppings:
Chopped green bell peppers
Chopped onion (or thinly sliced onion rings)
Sliced fresh or canned mushrooms
Sliced olives
Fat-free mozzarella cheese, shredded
Fat-free Parmesan cheese, grated

MAKES
TWO 12-
INCH
PIZZAS

3 GRAMS FAT

Prep :10
Cook :45
Stand :00
Total :55

Place the rolled-out pizza dough on baking sheets that have been sprayed with vegetable oil cooking spray.

Mix the sauce ingredients with 1 cup of water and simmer for short time. Pour on crust. Top with any or all desired toppings. (Add turkey sausage, cooked and drained, or 98% fat-free ham, shredded, if desired.)

Bake in a 400 degree oven about 45 minutes, or until veggies and crust are done.

PIZZA MEXICANA

SERVES 2

2 GRAMS FAT

Prep :10
Cook :07
Stand :00
Total :17

1 (16-ounce) can refried beans, fat-free
1 (12-inch) pizza crust (page 114), prebaked
³/₄ cup salsa, chunky mild or medium
¼ cup shredded fat-free Monterey jack cheese
¼ cup shredded fat-free Cheddar cheese
1 cup assorted fresh vegetables (sliced peppers, mushrooms, etc.)
¼ cup sliced green onions
1 (2-ounce) can black olives, drained and sliced
1 tablespoon minced cilantro (optional)

Preheat the oven to 450 degrees.

Spread the beans evenly over the cooked pizza crust, then spread with the salsa. Mix the cheeses together. Sprinkle over the salsa. Top with the vegetables, green onions, and olives.

Bake for 7 to 10 minutes, or until the cheese is melted. Garnish with cilantro if desired.

STOVE-TOP PIZZA

SERVES 2

2 GRAMS FAT

Prep :10
Cook :20
Stand :00
Total :30

2 cups Stove Top stuffing, any flavor
2 tablespoons Butter Buds liquid
²/₃ cup hot water
Spaghetti sauce
Sliced or chopped vegetables
Fat-free mozzarella cheese, shredded

Mix the stuffing, Butter Buds, and water and stir until moistened. Spread evenly in 9-inch round pan, pressing lightly to form shape of pan.

Pour low-fat spaghetti sauce over evenly. Top with any desired veggies, sautéed in water until tender.

Bake at 350 degrees for 15 minutes before topping with fat-free mozzarella cheese. Bake about 5 minutes longer to melt cheese.

Variation: Double the amount of Butter Buds and stuffing, and use a 9 x 13 x 2-inch dish for serving 6.

Vegetables

PINEAPPLE-
STUFFED ACORN SQUASH

SERVES 6

0 GRAMS FAT
(2 GRAMS
EACH IF
PECANS USED)

Prep :15
Cook 1:00
Stand :00
Total 1:15

3 medium acorn squash
1 (8-ounce) can crushed pineapple in juice
$\frac{1}{3}$ cup firmly packed brown sugar
$\frac{1}{4}$ cup pecans, chopped (optional)
3 tablespoons Butter Buds
$\frac{1}{2}$ teaspoon ground cinnamon

Preheat the oven to 375 degrees.

Cut the squash in half lengthwise and remove the seeds. Set aside.

Combine the pineapple, brown sugar, pecans, Butter Buds, and cinnamon in a medium bowl. Mix well. Spoon some of the pineapple mixture into each squash half. Arrange in a 9 x 13 x 2-inch baking dish; pour $\frac{3}{4}$ cup of water into the dish. Cover with foil and bake for 50 minutes. Uncover and bake 10 minutes longer.

BAKED BEANS

SERVES 10

1 GRAM FAT

Prep :15
Cook 1:30
Stand :00
Total 1:45

This is an excellent picnic or church-function recipe but you can halve it and use it just for your family. It has more of a barbecue taste than sweet.

1 (1-gallon) can pinto beans (just drain off if any fat has collected)
1 cup chopped celery
1 cup chopped onion
1 cup chopped green bell pepper
$\frac{1}{2}$ cup honey
1 cup salsa
$\frac{3}{4}$ cup cubed 98% fat-free ham
$\frac{1}{4}$ cup prepared mustard

Mix all ingredients well and bake uncovered in a large casserole about 1½ to 2 hours at 350 degrees. Stir once midway.

BAKED BEAN STORY

I created my recipe for baked beans in the days when my aunts were coming in the summer. Dad had seven sisters, and they would all come to see him at the same time in the summer and stay at my house (which could be called Roadway Inn or Do Drop In). They are all old and either gone or in nursing homes, including Dad, except three. No more summer get-togethers. We always had a big cookout and party. One aunt from Louisiana would bring shrimp, oysters, and crawfish. My brother did the steaks, and I did the down-home country cooking—not always fat-free until the last two years. The Washington aunt would bring apples and onions. California aunt would bring English walnuts, figs, oranges, lemons, etc. New Mexico brought a thirst. You should see some of the pictures of the preparation going on for one of these parties. Aunts all over the cabinets cooking all kinds of things. Mom was the hush puppy queen; my sister-in-law inherited that title. My brother was the fry captain for the fish, which came out of my dad's catfish pond. Sometimes there would be thirty or more of us.

We would even have themes. My cousin from Louisiana brought Cajun music and we would be dancing on the patio or driveway, wherever we were cooking. We had big cookers that we would cook in outside. These are stories that need to be remembered and I am sure that we will all do just that. I just wanted to share with you that this type of thing really happened and still happens. Do some of the same type of getting together with your family. It is worth the effort.

> Beans are packed with protein, low in fat and cholesterol. Beans are one of the best sources of complex carbohydrates and dietary fiber. Beans contain more fiber per serving than most vegetables, fruits, grains, or cereals. A diet high in fiber has been linked to lowering cholesterol, maintaining blood sugar levels for body energy, and curbing the hunger bug.

THREE BEAN BAKE

SERVES 4

1 GRAM FAT

Prep :10
Cook :30
Stand :00
Total :40

1 (16-ounce) can Great Northern beans, drained
1 (16-ounce) can spicy chili beans, undrained
1 (16-ounce) can light or dark kidney beans, drained
¹/₂ cup ketchup
¹/₃ cup firmly packed brown sugar
¹/₂ teaspoon ginger

Combine all the ingredients and mix well. Place in an uncovered casserole and bake at 350 degrees for 30 to 40 minutes, until thoroughly heated. Stir a couple of times during the baking period.

BROCCOLI CORN CASSEROLE

SERVES 2

0 GRAMS FAT

Prep :15
Cook :45
Stand :00
Total 1:00

1 (10-ounce) package frozen chopped broccoli, defrosted
1 (16-ounce) can cream-style corn
¹/₂ cup crushed fat-free crackers, divided
¹/₄ cup egg substitute
1 tablespoon instant minced onion
¹/₂ teaspoon salt
Dash of pepper
4 tablespoons Butter Buds, divided

Heat the oven to 350 degrees. Spray a 1-quart casserole dish with vegetable oil cooking spray.

Combine the broccoli and corn with ¹/₄ cup of the cracker crumbs, the egg substitute, minced onion, salt, pepper, and 2 tablespoons of the Butter Buds. Turn into the prepared casserole.

Mix the remaining ¹/₄ cup cracker crumbs and 2 tablespoons Butter Buds. Sprinkle on top. Bake for 45 minutes.

BAKED CAJUN CABBAGE

1 large head cabbage

Cheese Sauce:
1 cup chopped onion
1 cup chopped celery
1 cup chopped green pepper
Salt
Cayenne pepper
1½ cups skim milk
3 tablespoons cornstarch
½ pound fat-free Cheddar cheese, shredded (2 cups)

Topping:
1 cup chopped green onions
¼ cup seasoned Italian bread crumbs

SERVES 6

0 GRAMS FAT

Prep :15
Cook :50
Stand :00
Total 1:05

Heat the oven to 350 degrees.

Remove the outer leaves and core from the cabbage. Cut into bite-size sections. Cook uncovered in a large pot of boiling water about 10 minutes or until tender crisp. Drain in a colander.

Make the cheese sauce: In a separate saucepan, sauté the onions, celery, and green pepper in ¼ cup water. Add the salt and cayenne pepper and sauté for about 10 minutes. Add the milk, blending well. Mix the cornstarch with ½ cup of cold water; add to the saucepan and stir in until creamy. Add the cheese. Stir until smooth.

Place the cabbage in a 2-quart casserole. Top with the cheese sauce. Sprinkle with the green onions and bread crumbs. Bake for about 30 minutes.

When cooking cauliflower, squirt in a little lemon juice to keep it from turning dark.

MEXICAN CABBAGE

SERVES 2

0 GRAMS FAT

Prep :10
Cook :06
Stand :00
Total :16

1 large onion, sliced thin
1 large head cabbage, trimmed of large outer leaves and cored
1 can Rotel tomatoes and green chiles
³/₄ teaspoon salt
2 tablespoons vinegar (optional)

Place onions in the bottom of a microwave-safe serving bowl. Quarter the cabbage and place over the onions. Pour the tomatoes and green chiles on top of the cabbage. Sprinkle salt and vinegar over all.

Cover and bake in the microwave on Medium heat for 3 minutes. Stir and cook 3 more minutes. (Time may vary according to your microwave oven.) Serve hot.

CORN AND LIMA BEANS

SERVES 2

0 GRAMS FAT

Prep :05
Cook :15
Stand :00
Total :20

¹/₃ cup low-fat reduced-sodium chicken broth
1 cup frozen or canned baby lima beans
1 cup frozen or canned corn
¹/₄ teaspoon sugar
¹/₈ teaspoon black pepper
2 tablespoons fat-free sour cream

Bring the broth to a boil. Add the beans and corn, return to a boil, reduce the heat, and cover. Simmer for 8 to 10 minutes, or until vegetables are just tender. If canned vegetables are used, adjust the time.

Add the sugar and pepper. Simmer uncovered until the liquid is almost evaporated. Stir in the sour cream and serve.

Cooking cabbage can be pretty smelly. Next time put a heel of bread on top of the cabbage before putting the lid on. When all is done (throw away the cabbage and eat the bread. Ha! Ha! I was only teasing), throw away the bread and the smell at the same time. This also works for broccoli and brussels sprouts. (My mom used to say to cook wild duck, place an apple and an onion in the pot with the duck to cook; when done, throw away the duck and eat the apple and the onion. The cabbage tease reminded me of this.)

CORN PUDDING

1¼ cups egg substitute
1 egg white
1 cup skim milk
2 tablespoons flour
¼ teaspoon baking powder
⅛ teaspoon black pepper
1⅓ cups fresh or frozen whole-kernel corn
2 green onions, including tops, chopped
2 teaspoons fat-free Parmesan cheese

SERVES 4

0 GRAMS FAT

Prep :15
Cook 1:15
Stand :00
Total 1:30

Preheat the oven to 350 degrees. Spray a 9-inch deep-dish pie pan with vegetable oil cooking spray.

In a large bowl, whisk together the egg substitute, egg white, milk, flour, baking powder, and pepper. Stir in the corn, green onions, and cheese.

Transfer the mixture to the prepared pan. Set the pie pan in a large shallow baking pan. Add enough water to the baking pan to come halfway up the sides of the pie pan.

Bake uncovered for 1 to 1¼ hours, or until a knife inserted halfway between the side and center comes out clean and the pudding is puffed and golden.

SCALLOPED CORN

SERVES 4

0 GRAMS FAT

Prep :15
Cook :40
Stand :00
Total :55

¹/₄ cup chopped onion
¹/₄ cup chopped green bell pepper
1 egg white, slightly beaten
¹/₂ cup crushed fat-free saltine crackers, divided
¹/₂ cup skim milk
¹/₈ teaspoon seasoned salt
¹/₈ teaspoon pepper
1 (8-ounce) can whole-kernel corn
1 (8-ounce) can cream-style corn
1 teaspoon fat-free margarine, melted

Preheat the oven to 350 degrees. Coat a 1-quart casserole with vegetable oil cooking spray.

In a medium saucepan, sauté the onion and green pepper in a small amount of water until crisp-tender. Drain.

In a large mixing bowl, stir together the egg white, ¹/₄ cup of the crackers crumbs, the milk, seasoned salt, and pepper. Add the cooked onion and peppers, the whole-kernel corn, and the cream-style corn. Mix thoroughly.

Pour the corn mixture into the prepared casserole. In a small bowl toss the remaining ¹/₄ cup cracker crumbs with the melted margarine. Sprinkle over the corn mixture.

Bake for about 35 to 40 minutes, or until a knife inserted near the center comes out clean. Let stand for 5 to 10 minutes before

When peeling onions cut the root end off last and you won't be in tears so much. Soaking onion in ice water also takes out some of the strength.

> Choose bright orange carrots—they will have more vitamin A than paler ones.

CORN TAMALE PIE

1 cup yellow cornmeal
$^1/_3$ cup sugar
1 tablespoon baking powder
$^1/_2$ teaspoon salt
1 (16-ounce) carton fat-free cottage cheese
1 (16-ounce) package frozen petite corn kernels, thawed, or 2 cups canned shoepeg corn, drained
3 green onions, chopped
4 egg whites, at room temperature
2 (14-ounce) cans Mexican-style stewed tomatoes

SERVES 4

0 GRAMS FAT

Prep :20
Cook 1:00
Stand :10
Total 1:30

Preheat the oven to 350 degrees. Spray an 8-inch square glass baking dish with vegetable oil cooking spray.

In a large bowl, combine the cornmeal, sugar, baking powder, and salt. Whisk to blend. Mix in the cottage cheese, then the corn and green onions.

In a separate bowl, beat the egg whites until stiff but not dry. Fold the whites into the cornmeal mixture in 2 additions.

Transfer the batter to the prepared dish. Bake until the top is golden and feels firm in the center, about 50 minutes. Let stand 10 minutes.

While the tamale pie is baking, make a tomato sauce: Boil the stewed tomatoes uncovered in a heavy saucepan until reduced to sauce consistency, about 10 minutes.

Cut the tamale pie into squares and leave in the baking dish. Spoon tomato sauce over and serve.

HOMINY CASSEROLE

SERVES 4

LESS THAN 1
GRAM FAT

Prep :10
Cook :30
Stand :00
Total :40

2 cans hominy, drained
1 (8-ounce) carton fat-free sour cream
1 (4-ounce) can chopped green chiles
¹/₄ cup grated fat-free Parmesan cheese

Preheat the oven to 350 degrees. Lightly coat a baking dish with vegetable oil cooking spray.

In a large bowl, combine the hominy with the sour cream and chiles. Mix thoroughly and put in the baking dish. Sprinkle grated cheese over the top. Cover and bake for 30 minutes. Serve hot.

SPICY MUSHROOMS

SERVES 4

0 GRAMS FAT

Prep :05
Cook :00
Stand 4:00
Total 4:05

¹/₂ cup fat-free Italian dressing
1 teaspoon crushed dried basil
4 cups fresh mushrooms, sliced

Mix the dressing and basil in a glass bowl. Stir in the mushrooms. Cover and refrigerate at least 4 hours, stirring occasionally.

Tomatoes

You always have a little flower bed space in your yard and nothing is nicer than to be able to pick a fresh tomato from your very own vine. Plant a few—you will really enjoy them.

Plant a few sprigs of dill near your tomato plant to keep worms away from your tomatoes.

I always thought that you should turn your tomatoes stem down and put in a sunlit place to finish ripening. Not true. Leave them with their stems up and in a spot *out* of the sunlight to ripen. Do not refrigerate your tomatoes; it will make them mushy,

STEWED TOMATOES AND OKRA

2 cups okra, frozen sliced or fresh
$1/2$ cup chopped onion
$1/2$ cup chopped green bell pepper
2 (8-ounce) cans tomatoes
1 tablespoon lemon juice
1 teaspoon crushed oregano
$1/4$ teaspoon salt
$1/4$ teaspoon bottled hot pepper sauce, or to taste

SERVES 4

0 GRAMS FAT

Prep :10
Cook :17
Stand :00
Total :27

Remove tip and stem ends from fresh okra and cut into $1/4$-inch slices.

Sauté the onion and green pepper in $1/4$ cup water in a large skillet for about 2 minutes, stirring constantly. Add the okra, tomatoes, lemon juice, oregano, salt, and hot pepper sauce. Cover and cook over medium low heat 15 to 20 minutes, or until okra is tender.

HOBO CASSEROLE

SERVES 6

LESS THAN 1
GRAM FAT IN
ENTIRE DISH

Prep :30
Cook :40
Stand :00
Total 1:10

Beans:
1 cup chopped onion
$^1/_2$ cup chopped green pepper
2 cloves garlic, chopped fine
1 (14-ounce) can kidney beans, drained
1 (14-ounce) can pinto beans, drained
1 (16-ounce) can tomatoes, chopped, juice and all
1 (8-ounce) can tomato sauce
1 teaspoon chili powder
$^1/_2$ teaspoon prepared mustard
$^1/_8$ teaspoon hot pepper sauce

Corn Bread:
1 cup yellow cornmeal
1 cup all-purpose flour
$2^1/_2$ teaspoons baking powder
$^1/_2$ teaspoon salt
1 tablespoon sugar
1 cup skim milk
$^1/_2$ cup egg substitute
1 tablespoon canola oil (optional)
1 (8-ounce) can cream-style corn

Preheat the oven to 375 degrees.

Spray a large skillet with vegetable oil cooking spray, and sauté the onion, green pepper, and garlic 3 to 5 minutes, or until tender. (Add $^1/_4$ cup water if desired.) Stir in the beans, tomatoes, tomato sauce, chili powder, mustard, and hot sauce. Cover and cook 5 minutes. Pour into a 9 x 13 x 2-inch baking dish. Set aside.

Mix the corn bread: Combine the cornmeal and flour with the baking powder, salt, and sugar. In a separate bowl, mix the milk, egg substitute, oil, and corn. Stir into the dry ingredients until combined.

Spoon the corn bread mixture evenly over the bean mixture to within 1 inch of the edge all around.

Bake for 30 to 35 minutes, or until the corn bread is golden. Serve hot.

SWEET POTATO PUFF

3 cups sliced carrots
1 (16-ounce) can cut sweet potatoes in light syrup, drained
¹/₄ cup firmly packed brown sugar
2 tablespoons unsweetened orange juice
¹/₂ teaspoon ground cinnamon
¹/₈ teaspoon salt
¹/₄ teaspoon vanilla extract

SERVES 4

0.3 GRAM FAT

Prep :15
Cook :35
Stand :00
Total :50

Preheat the oven to 350 degrees. Spray a 9-inch square baking dish with vegetable oil cooking spray.

Cook the carrot slices in boiling water to cover for 15 minutes, or until very tender; drain.

Fit a food processor with the steel blade. Turn the carrots into the processor bowl along with the sweet potatoes, brown sugar, orange juice, cinnamon, salt, and vanilla. Process until smooth; scrape down sides as needed.

Spoon the sweet potato mixture into the prepared dish, spreading it evenly. Bake uncovered for 20 to 25 minutes.

Variation: Marshmallow creme may be dotted on top. Bake 5 minutes longer.

> When storing carrots, be sure to take off the tops. They drain out all the moisture from them and make them limp. You can revive them sometimes by soaking in very cold water.

VEGETABLE CHILI

SERVES 6

0 GRAMS FAT

Prep :30
Cook 1:15
Stand :00
Total 1:45

1 cup chopped onion
1 cup chopped celery
1 cup chopped green pepper
1 clove garlic, chopped
1¹/₂ cups chopped zucchini
1 (14-ounce) can low-sodium stewed tomatoes
1 (14-ounce) can tomato sauce
1 package chili seasoning, such as McCormick
2 cans kidney beans (or your favorite beans even leftover) (I like to use chili beans, canned)

Cover the bottom of a large saucepan with 3 or 4 tablespoons of water. Add the chopped onion, celery, green pepper, and garlic. Sauté until wilted, 3 to 4 minutes. Add the zucchini and cook until tender, 5 to 10 minutes.

Add the tomatoes, juice and all, the tomato sauce, chili seasoning, and beans. Simmer for about 1 hour, just as you would any chili.

When Vidalia onions are in season I buy up several pounds and store in an old refrigerator we have in the garage for drinks and veggies. They will keep all winter long. Just be sure they are nice and dry before storing them. At Christmas time I always have nice Vidalia onions.

> Lettuce leaves absorb fat. Place several on top of your stew pot or whatever you are cooking and watch the fat cling to them.

VEGETABLE GUMBO

Serve this on a bed of rice, or add cooked macaroni and serve with a salad and garlic toast.

SERVES 4

1 onion, chopped
1 clove garlic, chopped
1 (14½-ounce) can stewed Italian tomatoes, juice and all
1 (16-ounce) package vegetable gumbo mix
Salt and pepper to taste
Dash of cayenne pepper

0 GRAMS FAT

Prep :10
Cook :33
Stand :00
Total :43

Sauté onion and garlic in ¼ cup water for 2 or 3 minutes. Add tomatoes, vegetable mix, and ½ tomato can of water. Simmer 30 minutes, or until tender. Season with salt, pepper, and cayenne.

> Cabbage, kale, turnip, spinach, mustard greens, brussels sprouts, broccoli—all of these vegetables are good cancer fighters. Try to include at least one of them in your diet several times a week.

VEGETABLE SOUFFLÉ IN PEPPER CUPS

SERVES 6

0 GRAMS FAT

Prep :15
Cook :40
Stand :00
Total :55

1 cup chopped broccoli
$^1/_2$ cup shredded carrot
$^1/_4$ cup chopped onion
1 teaspoon diced basil leaves, or $^1/_3$ teaspoon dried
$^1/_2$ teaspoon black pepper
2 tablespoons cornstarch
1 $^1/_4$ cups skim milk
1 (8-ounce) container egg substitute
3 large green peppers, cored and halved lengthwise

Heat the oven to 375 degrees.

In a nonstick skillet sauté the broccoli, carrot, onion, basil, and black pepper in $^1/_4$ cup water until limp and brightly colored, 3 to 5 minutes. Dissolve the Stir in the cornstarch in $^1/_4$ cup of the cold skim milk. Gradually add the remaining 1 cup of milk, stirring constantly over medium heat until thickened. Remove from heat; set aside.

In a medium bowl, with an electric mixer at high speed, beat the egg substitute until foamy. Gently fold into the broccoli mixture; spoon into the pepper halves. Place in a baking dish. Bake for 30 to 35 minutes, or until a knife inserted near the center comes out clean. Serve immediately with a nice green salad.

> Vegetables are so good for you; try just cooking them plain with no seasoning. And try not to overcook them and lose so much of their flavor. Cook them crisp-tender. I have learned to appreciate the flavor of so many vegetables since I have cut out the fat, which was used for flavor. They have their very own special taste.

ZUCCHINI PATTIES

3¹/₂ cups grated zucchini (about 1 pound)
2 tablespoons grated onion
2 tablespoons chopped parsley
¹/₃ cup fat-free Parmesan cheese
1 cup soft fresh bread crumbs
³/₄ teaspoon salt
¹/₄ teaspoon pepper
¹/₂ cup egg substitute
Fine dry bread crumbs (packaged)

SERVES 6

LESS THAN
1 GRAM FAT
EACH

Prep :20
Cook :30
Stand :00
Total :50

Heat the oven to 350 degrees. Spray a cookie sheet with vegetable oil cooking spray.

After grating the zucchini, squeeze out as much liquid as possible with your hands. Combine the zucchini, onion, parsley, cheese, and 1 cup of soft bread crumbs with the salt, pepper, and egg substitute. Shape into patties and coat with dry bread crumbs.

Place on the cookie sheet, then lightly spray the patties with cooking spray. Bake for 30 to 40 minutes, or until golden brown.

Potatoes

POTATO STORY

I have many fond memories of potato planting time and digging them with my dad. Planting is quite a job. You have to cut the potatoes into chunks with an eye on each chunk; that is what sprouts and makes them grow. The seed potatoes are covered with dirt, as they have never been cleaned or washed. (They are just going to go back into the dirt so why wash them? Well believe me it takes several days of scrubbing before your hands look like they are clean again.) You get the starchy juice from inside and the dirt from the outside mixed and now you have a dirt paste on your hands.

Your ground has to be hilled up and a hole dug in each hill. Then you go along carrying this heavy bucket full of potatoes you have cut, not to mention that you have several fingers bleeding by this time. You drop a potato in each hill, then you cover them with dirt. Now you wait for time to do its thing along with the fertilizer and watering and weeding.

You get the prettiest bushes of nice green that comes up and they start to spread out and pretty soon they are solid rows of nice greenery. Sometimes Dad's would be knee high. He was some kind of great farmer.

The time has come for the fun—you get to dig under the vines to find the potatoes. What you find is such fun, maybe a little tiny one, maybe a half dozen big ones, but early in the season you get to use the tiny ones for several things. My favorite is green (garden) peas and new potatoes with white gravy. This was always one of the first things you got to eat from the garden in the spring as the green peas are also early. My mom could make the best "peas and taters" in the world bar none.

Now is time for the work to strike again. You have to dig all the hills of potatoes now and pick them up. Carry the heavy buckets of big potatoes somewhere and spread them out so that they will not rot and can get air and dry. Dad always planted such a large garden that it took the whole family to pick potatoes. We would have home-grown potatoes all summer long and store some inside when it came time for the winter to set in so they wouldn't freeze.

I use potatoes in many of my recipes. I know that you will enjoy them, most of all because they are so good for you, but just think of how easy it was to go to the grocery store and "pick potatoes." I bet the price of potatoes doesn't bother you near as much as before you read my "Potato Story," does it? If you think that was bad I could raise the hair on the back of your neck with some pork tales.

POTATO BOATS

SERVES 4

0 GRAMS FAT

Prep :30
Cook 1:10
Stand :00
Total 1:40

2 baking potatoes
2 ounces fat-free cream cheese, softened
2 tablespoons minced chives
$^1/_4$ teaspoon dried basil, crushed
$^1/_8$ teaspoon salt
Dash of pepper
3 to 4 tablespoons skim milk
Paprika

Scrub potatoes and prick with a fork. Bake in a preheated 375 degree oven for about 45 to 50 minutes, depending on the size of potatoes, or until tender.

Cut potatoes in half lengthwise. Gently scoop out each potato half, leaving a thin shell. Set shells aside.

Place the pulp in mixing bowl, add softened and cubed cream cheese, chives, basil, salt, and pepper. Beat until smooth. Add milk a little at a time, beating until potato mixture is fluffy.

Spoon the mixture back into the potato shells. Sprinkle with paprika. Place on a baking sheet, cover loosely with foil, and bake for 10 minutes. Uncover and bake an additional 10 minutes.

Variations: You may choose many variations to these boats. Use sour cream instead of cream cheese. Use fat-free Cheddar cheese in and on top of the potatoes. Use your imagination and add your favorite toppings or herbs and spices. You can even make an entire meal with these by adding steamed broccoli, or one or more other vegetables.

COMPANY TATERS

5 to 6 medium baking potatoes
2 cups fat-free sour cream
1 teaspoon cornstarch
³/₄ cup chopped green onions
1¹/₂ cups shredded fat-free Cheddar cheese
1¹/₂ teaspoons salt
1 teaspoon pepper
Paprika

SERVES 8

0 GRAMS FAT

Prep :20
Cook 1:30
Stand 4:00
Total 5:50

Preheat the oven to 350 degrees.

Boil the potatoes, jackets on, in water to cover, for 35 minutes or until tender. Cool. Peel and grate.

In a medium bowl, combine the sour cream, cornstarch, green onions, Cheddar cheese, salt, and pepper. Mix well. Add the grated potatoes and spoon the mixture into a 9 x 13 x 2-inch baking dish. Cover and refrigerate for 3 to 4 hours or overnight.

Bake for 40 to 50 minutes. Sprinkle with paprika and serve.

Potatoes were one of the first things that we thought we had to give up years ago when we thought of losing weight or going on a diet. The potato is not what is fattening—it is the way it is prepared and the things that we put on the potato: sour cream and butter. Nowadays, the facts are out and we can start with the potato and build a meal around it.

CONFETTI POTATOES

SERVES 6

VERY LOW-FAT

Prep :15
Cook :40
Stand :00
Total :55

$^1/_2$ cup chopped onion
1 (16-ounce) package frozen hash brown potatoes
1 (10-ounce) can Healthy Request cream of mushroom soup
1 soup can skim milk
1 cup shredded fat-free Cheddar cheese
1 small green pepper, cored and chopped
2 tablespoons chopped pimiento
1 cup cheese-cracker crumbs (I use Cheese Nips, which have less fat)

Preheat the oven to 375 degrees.

In a nonstick skillet sauté the onion in about $^1/_4$ cup water for 3 to 5 minutes, until tender. Stir in the potatoes, soup, and milk. Add the cheese, green pepper, and pimiento and $^1/_2$ cup of the cheese crackers.

Pour into shallow casserole and top with the remaining cracker crumbs.

Bake uncovered for 35 to 40 minutes, until bubbly.

POTATO CONFETTI CASSEROLE

A good do-ahead dish.

SERVES 6

LESS THAN 1
GRAM FAT

Prep :20
Cook 1:00
Stand :30
Total 1:50

3 pounds medium potatoes, peeled and quartered
$^1/_2$ cup Butter Buds liquid
2 (3-ounce) packages fat-free cream cheese, softened
1 cup shredded fat-free Cheddar cheese
1 (2-ounce) jar diced pimientos, drained
1 small green pepper, chopped fine
1 bunch green onions, chopped fine
$^1/_2$ cup grated fat-free Parmesan cheese
$^1/_4$ cup skim milk
1 teaspoon salt

Cook potatoes in boiling water to cover for 15 to 20 minutes, or until tender. Drain and mash. Add Butter Buds and cream cheese.

Beat with an electric mixer until smooth. Stir in ½ cup of the Cheddar cheese, the pimientos, green pepper, onions, Parmesan, milk, and salt. Spoon into a lightly sprayed baking dish (11 x 7 x 1½) that has been lightly sprayed with vegetable oil cooking spray. Cover and chill if desired.

The next day, or when you are ready to bake the casserole, remove it from the refrigerator and let stand 30 minutes. Bake uncovered in a preheated 350 degree oven for 40 minutes, or until thoroughly heated. Sprinkle with the remaining ½ cup of Cheddar cheese. Bake 5 minutes longer, or until the cheese melts.

FAKE FRENCH FRIES

Serve these potatoes right away since they lose their crispness quickly.

SERVES
2 TO 4

LESS THAN 1 GRAM FAT PER SERVING

3 large unpeeled potatoes, scrubbed and patted dry
1 tablespoon canola oil
½ teaspoon salt

Preheat the oven to 400 degrees. Cut the potatoes into sticks about the size of french fries. Put them in a bowl with the oil and salt. Toss them well. Spread them on a baking sheet and bake until golden brown and tender, about 25 minutes.

Prep :10
Cook :25
Stand :00
Total :35

Low-Fat Pan Fries
For pan fries without all the fat try using steamed or baked potatoes, sliced thin. Spray a nonstick skillet and dry fry at a medium high heat. Spray the tops of the potatoes a couple of times after stirring them. This will satisfy your fry craving and your figure.

Keep potatoes cool but not cold and in a dark place. Refrigeration converts the potato starch into sugar, creating a sweet taste and causing potatoes to darken prematurely while cooking.

HASH BROWN CASSEROLE

SERVES 8

LESS THAN 1
GRAM FAT

Prep :14
Cook 1:16
Stand :00
Total 1:30

1 1/2 cups chopped onion
3 tablespoons flour
1/2 teaspoon dry mustard
1/4 teaspoon salt
1 1/2 cups skim milk
1/2 cup low-sodium chicken broth
1 1/2 cups shredded fat-free Cheddar cheese
3/4 cup fat-free shredded Swiss cheese
1/2 teaspoon pepper
1 cup fat-free sour cream
1 (32-ounce) package frozen Southern-style hash brown potatoes, thawed
Paprika

Preheat the oven to 350 degrees. Spray a 9 x 13 x 2-inch baking dish with vegetable oil cooking spray. Set aside.

Coat a medium saucepan with vegetable oil cooking spray. Add the onion and sauté 3 to 5 minutes, until tender. Add the flour, mustard, and salt; stir well and cook 1 minute. Remove from the heat. Gradually add the milk and broth, stirring with a wire whisk until blended. Cook until thickened, stirring constantly. Remove from the heat; add the cheeses and pepper, stirring until cheeses melt. Stir in the sour cream.

Combine the cheese mixture and potatoes. Stir well. Spoon into the prepared baking dish. Sprinkle with paprika. Cover with foil and bake 35 minutes. Uncover and bake an additional 35 to 40 minutes.

To bring out the true flavor of a potato, bake it in its own skin. Foil locks in the moisture and gives you a boiled flavor. Pierce the skin before baking—have you ever cleaned an oven after one explodes? You won't ever forget to pierce one again. I had an all-chrome-inside oven when mine exploded the only time in my life that I failed to pierce one.

SCALLOPED POTATOES

¹/₄ cup nonfat dry milk powder
2 cups skim milk
2 tablespoons light margarine
¹/₄ cup all-purpose flour
¹/₂ teaspoon salt
¹/₂ teaspoon pepper
1³/₄ pounds potatoes, pared and cut into ¹/₄-inch-thick slices (about 4 potatoes)
1¹/₂ cups thinly sliced onions
³/₄ cup shredded fat-free Cheddar cheese
¹/₄ cup soft bread crumbs

SERVES 10

**2.9 GRAMS FAT
PER 1-CUP
SERVING**

Prep :15
Cook 1:16
Stand :00
Total 1:31

Coat a 12 x 8-inch casserole with vegetable oil cooking spray. Preheat the oven to 375 degrees.

Dissolve the milk powder in the skim milk and set aside. Melt the margarine in a heavy pan; add the flour and stir well. Cook over medium heat for 1 minute; it will be lumpy. Gradually add the milk, stirring constantly with a wire whisk until thickened. Add the salt and pepper. Remove the sauce from the heat.

Spread ¹/₄ cup of the sauce in the prepared baking dish; add half each of the potatoes, onions, and cheese, and spread with a layer of sauce. Repeat except for cheese. Cover and bake for 1 hour, or until the potatoes are tender. Uncover and sprinkle with the remaining cheese and bread crumbs. Coat lightly with cooking spray. Bake an additional 5 minutes.

Potatoes are good for you. They are loaded with vitamins B and C, have no fat or cholesterol, and are an excellent source of potassium, a medium potato containing 1½ times as much as a banana or cup of orange juice.

BUTTERMILK SCALLOPED POTATOES

The buttermilk bakes into a remarkably cheesy tasting sauce. Very simple to make.

SERVES 4

LESS THAN
3 GRAMS FAT

Prep :15
Cook 1:15
Stand :00
Total 1:30

¼ cup whole wheat flour
1 teaspoon salt
⅛ teaspoon pepper
2 large baking potatoes, peeled and sliced thin
2 tablespoons Butter Buds
1 medium onion, chopped
2 cups skim buttermilk (check the label; buy the 1 gram per cup)
Pinch of paprika

Preheat the oven to 350 degrees.

In a shallow dish combine the flour, salt, and pepper. Dredge the potatoes in the flour mixture and place them in a shallow 2-quart baking dish.

In a small skillet sprayed with vegetable oil cooking spray, sauté the onion for about 5 minutes, or until tender. Spoon the onion over the potatoes and pour buttermilk over top. Sprinkle paprika over potatoes and bake uncovered for 1 to 1¼ hours, or until the potatoes are tender.

WORKING WOMAN'S SCALLOPED POTATOES

1 package scalloped potato mix
1/3 cup chopped green onions
1/2 to 1 teaspoon Italian seasoning
1 1/2 cups boiling water
1 1/4 cups skim milk

Combine the dried potatoes, sauce mix, onions, and seasoning. Stir in the boiling water and milk; mix well. Turn into a casserole and bake at 375 to 400 degrees for 30 to 40 minutes.

SERVES 6

1 GRAM FAT
PER SERVING

Prep :05
Cook :40
Stand :00
Total :45

POTATO SPEARS

Serve with oven-fried fish or as appetizers with a fat-free sour cream.

3 to 4 large unpeeled baking potatoes, scrubbed and cut lengthwise into 8 wedges each
1 package onion soup mix (see Note)

Preheat the oven to 400 degrees.
Lightly spray the potato wedges with vegetable oil cooking spray. Put into a large plastic bag or bowl. Add the onion soup mix. Shake to coat potatoes. Arrange on a cookie sheet sprayed with cooking spray and bake until golden, 30 to 45 minutes.

Note: Read your labels. On the soup mix one has fat, one does not.

SERVES
2 TO 4

LESS THAN 1
GRAM FAT IN
ALL

Prep :10
Cook :30
Stand :00
Total :40

Avoid green-skinned potatoes; they have been exposed to the light too long. They are actually "sunburned." You can peel the green away, but if it is halfway into the potato throw it away.

BROCCOLI-STUFFED POTATOES

SERVES 6

LESS THAN 1 GRAM FAT IN ALL

Prep :10
Cook 1:19
Stand :00
Total 1:29

6 medium-size baking potatoes, scrubbed
1 teaspoon Butter Buds, liquid form
3 stalks broccoli (about 1 pound), stems peeled
1 cup shredded fat-free Cheddar cheese
1 1/4 cups skim milk
1 teaspoon salt
1/8 teaspoon black pepper

Preheat the oven to 400 degrees. Brush the skins of potatoes with Butter Buds and score them down the middle lengthwise. Bake for 45 to 60 minutes, or until tender.

Steam the broccoli for 6 to 8 minutes, or until just tender. Chop fine. Carefully slice the potatoes in half lengthwise and scoop the flesh into a bowl. Reserve the skins. Add the broccoli, 1/2 cup of the cheese, the milk, salt, and pepper to the potato. Mash until the mixture is pale green with dark flecks.

Spoon the mixture into the potato skins and sprinkle with the remaining cheese. Place on a baking sheet and bake for 10 minutes longer. Heat the broiler and broil the potatoes for 1 minutes, or until the tops are golden brown.

Breads

APPLE WHEAT MUFFINS

SERVES 12

LESS THAN 1 GRAM FAT EACH

Prep :15
Cook :20
Stand :05
Total :40

1 cup low-fat buttermilk
2 cups Wheaties cereal
$^1/_2$ cup finely chopped pared apple (about half a medium apple)
$^1/_4$ cup unsweetened apple juice
$^1/_4$ cup molasses
$^1/_4$ cup egg substitute
1 cup whole wheat flour
$^3/_4$ teaspoon baking soda
$^1/_4$ teaspoon salt
$^1/_4$ teaspoon cinnamon

Preheat the oven to 400 degrees. Line 12 muffin cups with paper baking cups. Spray with vegetable oil cooking spray.

Pour the buttermilk over the cereal in a medium bowl. Let stand 5 minutes, or until the cereal is soft. Add the chopped apple, the apple juice, molasses, and egg substitute; stir to combine.

In a small bowl, whisk together the flour, baking soda, salt, and cinnamon. Add the dry ingredients all at once to the cereal mixture; stir just until flour is moistened. The batter should be lumpy. Fill the muffin cups $^3/_4$ full.

Bake 20 minutes, or until a toothpick inserted in the center comes out *almost* clean. Immediately remove from pan.

BANANA BREAD

²/₃ cup sugar
¹/₄ cup reduced-fat margarine, softened
³/₄ cup egg substitute
1 cup mashed ripe bananas (about 2 large bananas)
1²/₃ cups flour
1 teaspoon baking soda
¹/₄ teaspoon baking powder
¹/₂ teaspoon salt

MAKES 1
LOAF (18
SLICES)

1 GRAM FAT
PER SLICE

Preheat the oven to 350 degrees. Spray an 8- or 9-inch loaf pan with vegetable oil cooking spray.

Beat the sugar and margarine in a medium bowl with an electric mixer until light and fluffy. And the egg substitute, bananas, and ¹/₄ cup of water. Beat on low speed until well blended.

Mix together the flour, baking soda, baking powder, and salt. Stir into the banana mixture just until moistened. Pour and scrape into the loaf pan.

Bake the 8-inch loaf for 60 minutes, the 9-inch for 45 to 50 minutes, or until a toothpick inserted in the center comes out clean.

Cool 5 minutes. Loosen sides of loaf from pan. Remove from pan and cool completely on a rack before slicing—if you can resist.

Prep :15
Cook 1:00
Stand :05
Total 1:20

Everyone probably knows that you ripen bananas by putting them in a paper sack, and that wrapping them in a wet towel will make them ripen even faster. But how in the world do you keep them from ripening so fast?

HOMEMADE BISCUITS

MAKES 8 THICK OR 12 THIN BISCUITS

1 GRAM FAT EACH

Prep :10
Cook :35
Stand :00
Total :45

3 cups self-rising flour
1 to 1¹/₂ cups skim milk, or enough to make a sticky dough

Preheat the oven to 400 degrees. Spray a baking sheet with vegetable oil cooking spray.

Put the flour in a bowl and add enough milk to make a sticky consistency (the stickier you can handle the dough the lighter the biscuits).

Turn out on a floured surface and knead just enough to make the dough workable. Pat out with fingers until thickness desired. (You can use a rolling pin but then you just have to clean it.) Cut out biscuits. Put in the sprayed pan. Spray the tops of the biscuits lightly; this will make them brown nice.

Bake thin biscuits for 12 to 15 minutes, or until golden brown. Thicker biscuits will take 35 to 40 minutes.

ALMOND SHORTCAKE BISCUITS

Serve with fresh strawberries.

MAKES 8 BISCUITS

7 GRAMS FAT EACH

Prep :15
Cook :15
Stand :00
Total :30

2¹/₄ cups all-purpose flour
¹/₃ cup sugar, plus 1 tablespoon for sprinkling over top
1¹/₂ teaspoons baking powder
³/₄ teaspoon baking soda
¹/₄ teaspoon salt
2 tablespoons light margarine, cold, cut into small pieces
³/₄ to 1 cup low-fat buttermilk (1 gram fat per cup)
1 tablespoon canola oil
¹/₂ teaspoon vanilla extract
¹/₈ teaspoon almond extract
1 tablespoon skim milk
¹/₄ cup sliced almonds

Heat the oven to 400 degrees. Spray a baking sheet with vegetable oil cooking spray; set aside.

Mix the flour, ¹/₃ cup of sugar, the baking powder, soda, and salt. Cut in the margarine until crumbly.

In a small bowl, combine ³/₄ cup of buttermilk, the oil, and the vanilla and almond extracts. Make a well in the center of the flour mixture. Add the buttermilk mixture. With a fork, stir just until combined, adding extra buttermilk if necessary to form a slightly sticky dough. Do *not* overmix.

Place the dough on a lightly floured surface and sprinkle with flour. Gently pat with fingertips to 1-inch thickness. Cut with a biscuit cutter. Place on the baking sheet. Brush with milk and sprinkle with the remaining tablespoon of sugar and the almonds. Bake for 10 to 15 minutes, until golden.

APPLE COFFEE CAKE

1 cup all-purpose flour
1¹/₂ teaspoons baking powder
¹/₂ teaspoon salt
³/₄ cup granulated sugar
¹/₃ cup skim milk
2 egg whites
¹/₃ cup light or dark corn syrup
2 medium apples, peeled and cut into ¹/₂-inch wedges
2 tablespoons cinnamon sugar

SERVES 4

FAT-FREE

Prep :15
Cook :50
Stand :00
Total 1:05

Spray a 9-inch round baking pan with vegetable oil cooking spray. Preheat the oven to 350 degrees.

In a large bowl, combine the flour, baking powder, and salt. In a medium bowl, using a wire whisk or fork, mix the granulated sugar and milk. Whisk in the egg whites and corn syrup. Gradually stir into the dry ingredients until smooth. Pour into the prepared pan.

Arrange the apples over the top, overlapping to cover. Sprinkle with cinnamon sugar. Bake for 50 minutes, or until a toothpick inserted in center comes out clean. Cool on a wire rack.

OVERNIGHT COFFEE CAKE
(DO AHEAD)

SERVES 8

1 GRAM FAT PER CAKE, IF NUTS OMITTED

Prep :10
Cook :35
Stand 8:00
Total 8:45

2 cups all-purpose flour
1 cup granulated sugar
1 cup firmly packed brown sugar, divided
1 teaspoon baking soda
1 teaspoon baking powder
$1/2$ teaspoon salt
2 teaspoons cinnamon, divided
1 cup low-fat buttermilk (1 gram fat per cup)
$2/3$ cup Butter Buds liquid
$1/2$ cup egg substitute
$1/2$ cup pecans, chopped (optional)

Preheat the oven to 350 degrees.

In a mixing bowl, combine the flour, granulated sugar, $1/2$ cup of the brown sugar, the baking soda, baking powder, salt, and 1 teaspoon of cinnamon. Add the buttermilk, Butter Buds, and egg substitute. Beat on low speed until the mixture is moistened, then beat on medium speed for 3 minutes.

Spoon into an oil-sprayed and floured 9 x 13 x 2-inch baking pan. Combine the remaining $1/2$ cup of brown sugar, the pecans, and 1 teaspoon of cinnamon. Sprinkle over the batter. Cover and refrigerate 8 to 12 hours.

Uncover and bake for 30 to 35 minutes, or until a toothpick inserted in the center comes out clean. Serve warm.

CORN BREAD

2 cups self-rising cornmeal (read the label—choose the 0-fat one)
$^1/_2$ cup egg substitute
1 cup skim milk, or enough to make a fairly stiff dough

SERVES 6

.05 GRAM
FAT PER
SERVING

Prep :10
Cook :35
Stand :00
Total :45

   Preheat the oven to 350 degrees. Spray an 8-inch baking pan or your cast-iron skillet with vegetable oil cooking spray.
   Put the cornmeal in a bowl and make a well in the center. Beat the egg substitute and milk together; pour into the cornmeal and stir until well mixed. Pour the batter into the prepared pan and bake until set in the middle. Spray the top of the corn bread with vegetable oil cooking spray. Continue to bake until golden brown and firm, about 35 minutes in all.

FRIED CORN BREAD

Quick and excellent.

2 cups self-rising cornmeal
$^1/_2$ cup egg substitute
Skim milk (enough to make a fairly heavy dough)

SERVES 8

.05 GRAM
FAT PER CAKE

Prep :05
Cook :15
Stand :00
Total :20

   Mix all the above ingredients. Drop by large spoonfuls on a hot nonstick skillet, like cooking pancakes. Turn when bubbles show on the top; cook until the other side is golden brown.

CHERRY-DATE QUICK BREAD

*A good make-ahead recipe. You may freeze
the loaf and store it for up to 3 months.*

SERVES 10

1 GRAM FAT
PER SLICE

Prep :15
Cook :40
Stand :10
Total 1:05

All-purpose flour
1 cup boiling water
³/₄ cup quick-cooking rolled oats
¹/₃ cup candied cherries
1 (16-ounce) package date bread mix
¹/₂ teaspoon grated nutmeg
¹/₄ cup egg substitute

Heat the oven to 375 degrees. Spray an 8 x 4-inch or 9 x 5-inch loaf pan with vegetable oil cooking spray. Sprinkle in a little flour to coat the pan, then tap out the excess flour.

Pour the boiling water over the oats and let stand 5 minutes. Chop the cherries and sprinkle with ¹/₂ teaspoon of flour; toss to coat.

Combine the bread mix, nutmeg, and egg substitute with ¹/₂ cup water. Add the oat mixture and the chopped cherries. Stir just until the dry ingredients are moistened. Pour into the greased and floured pan.

Bake for 35 to 40 minutes, or until the top of the loaf is deep golden brown. Cool 5 minutes before removing from pan. Turn out on a rack and cool completely.

CRANBERRY BREAD

2¹/₂ cups all-purpose flour
³/₄ cup sugar
2 tablespoons poppy seeds
1 tablespoon baking powder
1 cup skim milk
¹/₃ cup (5 tablespoons plus 1 teaspoon) fat-free margarine, melted
¹/₄ cup egg substitute
1 teaspoon vanilla extract
2 teaspoons grated lemon rind
1 cup fresh or frozen cranberries, chopped
Confectioners' sugar glaze (optional) (page 158)

SERVES 12

0 GRAMS FAT

Prep :15
Cook 1:10
Stand :10
Total 1:35

Heat the oven to 350 degrees. Spray the bottom of an 8¹/₂ x 4¹/₂ x 2¹/₂-inch loaf pan with vegetable oil cooking spray.

In large a bowl, mix the flour, sugar, poppy seeds, and baking powder. Mix the milk, margarine, egg substitute, vanilla, and lemon rind. Stir into the flour mixture just until moistened. Stir in cranberries; spoon into the prepared pan and smooth the top.

Bake for 60 to 70 minutes, or until a toothpick inserted near the center comes out clean. Cool in the pan for 10 minutes; then turn out on a wire rack and cool completely.

Cranberries: If you have trouble finding cranberries in your area other than at Thanksgiving and Christmastime, buy extra during the holidays and freeze them. You don't have to do anything except set them in the freezer in the bag you buy them in. They will keep for up to 6 months.

OVERNIGHT FRENCH TOAST

SERVES 8

1 GRAM FAT PER SLICE

Prep :10
Cook :08
Stand 8:00
Total 8:18

8 slices (³/₄ inch thick) French bread
1 cup egg substitute (equal to 4 eggs)
1 cup skim milk
1 tablespoon sugar
¹/₂ teaspoon vanilla extract
¹/₄ teaspoon cinnamon

Place bread in one layer in a 9 x 13 x 2-inch baking dish. Combine the egg substitute, milk, sugar, vanilla, and cinnamon. Beat well. Pour over the bread; turn each slice of bread to coat evenly. Cover and refrigerate up to 8 hours.

To serve: Heat a nonstick skillet and dry-fry the bread on both sides. Serve with hot syrup (light).

Cakes, Pies, and Cookies

Cakes

"THE BEST CAKE"

This is my number-one cake and best seller for the book. I hope you enjoy it just a tiny bit as much as I have.

SERVES 8

0 GRAMS FAT, IF NUTS OMITTED

Prep :15
Cook :40
Stand :10
Total 1:05

¹/₂ cup egg substitute
2 cups granulated sugar
2 cups all-purpose flour
2 teaspoons baking soda
1 (20-ounce) can crushed pineapple, juice and all (2¹/₂ cups)
1 teaspoon vanilla extract
1 cup nuts, chopped (optional)

Frosting:
1 (8-ounce) package fat-free cream cheese, softened
1¹/₂ cups confectioners' sugar
¹/₄ teaspoon vanilla extract

Heat the oven to 350 degrees. Spray a 9 x 13 x 2-inch pan with vegetable oil cooking spray.

Beat the egg substitute and granulated sugar together in an electric mixer. Mix the flour and baking soda; beat into the egg mixture. Add the pineapple, juice and all, and continue to mix, with mixer, until blended. Stir in the vanilla and nuts, if using.

Pour and scrape the batter into the prepared pan. Bake for 40 minutes.

Meantime, mix the frosting ingredients: Stir the cream cheese with a wire whisk, not with a mixer (fat-free cream cheese gets thin if beaten with a mixer). Gradually beat in the sugar, then stir in the vanilla.

Cool the cake about 10 minutes and frost. If frosting is thin, pour on the cake anyway; it is OK. Hot cake takes care of that.

You may sprinkle with additional nuts.

Sugar Tips: If you need to reduce your sugar, Sweet One granulated sugar substitute is very good. It is heat stable, which means it holds up well during cooking and baking without turning bitter.

In baked goods substitute a portion of the recipe's sugar with Sweet One; in recipes for sweetened beverages and sauces, you can replace all of the sugar with Sweet One.

APPLESAUCE CAKE

*Good with powdered sugar frosting or plain
with frozen yogurt (fat-free of course).*

SERVES 4

¹/₂ cup Butter Buds liquid
1 cup sugar
¹/₄ cup egg substitute
2 cups all-purpose flour
1 teaspoon salt
1 teaspoon baking soda
1 teaspoon baking powder
1 teaspoon ground cinnamon
¹/₂ teaspoon ground allspice
¹/₂ teaspoon ground nutmeg
¹/₄ teaspoon ground cloves
1 cup applesauce
³/₄ cup chopped nuts (optional)

0 GRAMS FAT
IN ENTIRE
DISH IF NUTS
OMITTED—8
GRAMS WITH
NUTS

Prep :15
Cook 1:00
Stand :05
Total 1:20

Preheat the oven to 350 degrees. Spray a 9-inch round cake pan with vegetable oil cooking spray.

Cream the Butter Buds and sugar until fluffy. Add the egg substitute and blend well. Whisk the dry ingredients together and add to the butter-sugar mixture in thirds, alternately with the applesauce. Fold in the nuts.

Pour into the prepared cake pan and bake for 50 to 60 minutes.

Cool in the pan for 5 minutes, then turn out of the pan and cool on a rack.

CHOCOLATE APPLESAUCE CAKE

SERVES 12

VERY LOW-FAT

Prep :15
Cook 1:00
Stand :10
Total 1:25

³/₄ cup Butter Buds liquid
1 cup firmly packed light brown sugar
¹/₂ cup granulated sugar
³/₄ cup egg substitute
1¹/₂ cups all-purpose flour
¹/₂ cup cocoa powder
1¹/₂ teaspoons baking soda
¹/₄ teaspoon salt
1³/₄ cups unsweetened applesauce
³/₄ cup chopped walnuts (optional)
1 cup (8 ounces) glazed whole red cherries, cut in halves (see Note)
1 cup (8 ounces) green glazed pineapple wedges, diced or coarsely chopped
¹/₄ cup (2 ounces) glazed diced orange peel, chopped

Glaze:
1¹/₂ cups confectioners' sugar
3 tablespoons skim milk

Heat the oven to 350 degrees. Spray a medium-size Bundt pan with vegetable oil spray and dust with flour.

Beat together the Butter Buds and sugars; add the egg substitute. In a separate bowl, mix together the flour, cocoa, baking soda, and salt. Beat into the butter-sugar mixture alternately with the applesauce, beginning and ending with dry ingredients. Stir in the walnuts, cherries, pineapple, and orange peel.

Pour the batter into the prepared pan and bake about 1 hour, until springy to the touch. Meantime, mix the ingredients for the glaze together. Cool the cake 10 minutes; remove from the pan. Cool. Drizzle with glaze and decorate with reserved cherries and pineapple pieces.

Note: Save a few cherries and pineapple pieces for decorating the top.

BLUEBERRY SCONE CAKE

1 (15-ounce) package nut or banana bread mix
⅓ cup low-fat buttermilk (1 gram fat per cup)
¼ cup egg substitute
1 cup fresh or frozen blueberries (do not thaw)
2 teaspoons sugar

SERVES 4

4 GRAMS FAT

Preheat the oven to 400 degrees. Spray a cookie sheet with vegetable oil cooking spray.

Combine the bread mix, buttermilk, and egg substitute. Stir 50 to 75 strokes by hand, just until the dry particles are moistened. Fold in the blueberries. Turn the dough onto the cookie sheet. Using floured fingers, shape into an 8-inch circle. Sprinkle with sugar.

Bake for 20 to 25 minutes, or until golden brown and a toothpick inserted into center comes out clean. Serve warm, cut into pie-shaped wedges.

Prep :10
Cook :25
Stand :00
Total :35

CHEESECAKE DELIGHT

1 cup graham cracker crumbs
¾ cup plus 3 tablespoons sugar
2 tablespoons fat-free margarine, melted
3 (8-ounce) packages Healthy Choice fat-free cream cheese, at room temperature
2 tablespoons flour
3 tablespoons lemon juice
¾ cup egg substitute
1 (8-ounce) carton nonfat lemon yogurt
Light whipped topping (optional)

SERVES 12

1 GRAM FAT
PER SERVING

Preheat the oven to 350 degrees.

Combine the graham cracker crumbs, 3 tablespoons of the sugar, and the margarine; mix well. Pat into the bottom of a 9-inch springform pan. Set aside.

Prep :15
Cook 1:10
Stand :00
Total 1:25

Mix the cream cheese, flour, and ³/₄ cup of sugar together with a wire whisk until fluffy and smooth. Gradually add the lemon juice and egg substitute. Beat well. Add the lemon yogurt and mix thoroughly. Pour over the prepared crust. Loosely place aluminum foil over the springform pan.

Bake for 60 to 70 minutes, or until the center of the cake is set. Gently run the tip of a knife between the cake and the edge of the pan. Cool the cake to room temperature before removing the rim of the pan. Chill. Serve with light whipped topping if desired.

NO-FAT CHOCOLATE CAKE

SERVES 12

3 GRAMS FAT

Prep :15
Cook :35
Stand :03
Total :53

1 cup evaporated (*not* sweetened condensed) skim milk
³/₄ cup cocoa powder
1 cup unsweetened applesauce
1 tablespoon vanilla extract
2 cups all-purpose flour
1¹/₂ cups sugar, divided
¹/₂ teaspoon baking powder
¹/₂ teaspoon baking soda
¹/₂ teaspoon salt
4 egg whites (large), at room temperature

Preheat the oven to 350 degrees. Spray two 9-inch round cake pans or one 9 x 13 x 2-inch pan with vegetable oil cooking spray and dust with flour.

Heat the evaporated milk in a medium-size saucepan until barely simmering. Remove from the heat and whisk in the cocoa until thickened and almost smooth (some tiny lumps will remain). Let stand 2 to 3 minutes to cool slightly. Whisk in the applesauce and vanilla extract.

Mix the flour, 1¹/₄ cups of the sugar, the baking powder, soda, and salt in a large bowl.

Beat the egg whites in a medium-size bowl with an electric mixer until thick and foamy. Gradually beat in the remaining

¼ cup of sugar and continue beating until stiff peaks form when the beaters are lifted.

Pour the cocoa mixture over the flour. Stir just until blended.

With a rubber spatula, gently stir about a quarter of the egg whites into the flour mixture. Fold in the remaining egg whites until no white streaks remain. Pour into the prepared pan or pans.

Bake for 25 to 30 minutes, or until a toothpick inserted near the center comes out clean and the edges begin to pull away from the sides.

Frost if desired with Easy Vanilla Frosting (page 162).

CHOCOLATE POTATO CAKE

2 cups sugar
2 cups leftover mashed potatoes (no-fat)
1 cup egg substitute
½ cup Butter Buds, liquid form
½ cup skim milk
1 tablespoon canola oil
2 cups all-purpose flour
6 tablespoons unsweetened cocoa powder
2 teaspoons baking powder
1 teaspoon ground cloves
1 teaspoon ground cinnamon
1 teaspoon grated nutmeg
1 teaspoon salt

SERVES
8 TO 10

1 GRAM FAT
PER SERVING

Prep :15
Cook :40
Stand :00
Total :55

Preheat the oven to 350 degrees. Lightly spray a 9 x 13 x 2-inch pan or two 8-inch round cake pans with vegetable oil cooking spray.

Put the sugar, mashed potatoes, egg substitute, Butter Buds, skim milk, and canola oil in a large bowl and beat with an electric mixer until smooth.

In a medium bowl, combine the flour, cocoa, baking powder,

cloves, cinnamon, nutmeg, and salt. Stir with a wire whisk until thoroughly mixed.

Add the dry ingredients to the wet ingredients and mix on low speed just enough to blend. Turn the batter into the prepared pan and bake for about 30 to 40 minutes, or until the top of the cake is springy to the touch. Cool in the pan on a wire rack.

EASY VANILLA FROSTING

2 egg whites, at room temperature
$^1/_2$ teaspoon cream of tartar
$^1/_4$ cup honey
2 teaspoons vanilla extract
1 cup instant nonfat dry milk powder, very fine textured

MAKES
ENOUGH
FROSTING
FOR A
9-INCH
2-LAYER
CAKE

0 GRAMS FAT

Prep :15
Cook :00
Stand :00
Total :15

In a clean, grease-free bowl, beat the egg whites until foamy. Add the cream of tartar and continue beating, adding the honey and vanilla. Gradually add the nonfat dry milk powder, beating constantly, until the frosting is a good spreading consistency.

CHOCOLATE CREAMY CUPCAKES

1 batch No-Fat Chocolate Cake batter (see recipe on page 160)
1 package (1-ounce serving size) instant French vanilla pudding
1³/₄ cups evaporated skim milk (*not* sweetened condensed)
Confectioners' sugar

Line 12 muffin tins with paper baking cups. Fill each with ⅓ cup batter. Bake 20 to 25 minutes at 350 degrees. Cool.

Prepare the pudding, using 1³/₄ cups evaporated skim milk instead of 2 cups whole milk. Refrigerate until set, about 1 hour.

With a thin sharp knife, slice off the tops of the cupcakes. Spread the bottoms with about 1½ tablespoons of pudding each. Replace tops.

Sprinkle with confectioners' sugar.

SERVES 12

1 GRAM FAT

Prep :10
Cook :25
Stand 1:00
Total 1:35

CREAM CHEESE BROWNIE CAKE

Cake Batter:
1½ cups all-purpose flour
1 cup sugar
½ teaspoon baking soda
¼ cup unsweetened cocoa powder
⅛ teaspoon salt
½ teaspoon vinegar
¼ cup fat-free mayonnaise
2 tablespoons light corn syrup
1 teaspoon vanilla extract

Cream Cheese Swirl:
⅓ cup fat-free cream cheese
1½ tablespoons sugar
¼ teaspoon vanilla extract

SERVES 6

LESS THAN 1
GRAM FAT

Prep :15
Cook :45
Stand :00
Total 1:00

Heat the oven to 350 degrees. Spray a 9-inch square baking dish with vegetable oil cooking spray.

In a large bowl, combine the flour, sugar, baking soda, cocoa, and salt. Stir until well blended. Add the vinegar, mayonnaise, corn syrup, vanilla, and 1 cup of water and mix with an electric mixer until smooth. Pour the cake batter into the prepared dish and set aside while making the cream cheese swirl.

In a small bowl, combine the cream cheese, sugar, and vanilla. Mix with an electric mixer until smooth and creamy. Drop about 1 tablespoon of the cream cheese mixture in 4 or 5 places on top of the cake batter.

Take a table knife, place the knife blade in the center of each cream cheese drop, and drag the cream cheese to make pretty swirls on top of the cake.

Bake for 40 to 45 minutes, until the cake is springy to the touch.

EASY CARROT CAKE

SERVES 10

VERY LOW-FAT

Prep :15
Cook :35
Stand :00
Total :50

1 box (2-layer) yellow cake mix, light
1¹/₄ cups fat-free salad dressing, such as Miracle Whip
1 cup egg substitute
2 teaspoons ground cinnamon
2 cups finely shredded carrots
¹/₂ cup chopped walnuts
Cream Cheese Frosting I (recipe follows)

Preheat the oven to 350 degrees. Spray a 9 x 13 x 2-inch baking dish with vegetable oil cooking spray.

Put the cake mix in a large bowl and add the salad dressing, egg substitute, cinnamon, and ¹/₄ cup of water. Beat on low speed with an electric mixer just until blended. Stir in the carrots and walnuts.

Pour the batter into the baking dish and bake for about 35 minutes, or until a wooden pick inserted near the center comes out clean.

When the cake is cool, frost with Cream Cheese Frosting I.

CREAM CHEESE FROSTING I

1 (3-ounce) package fat-free cream cheese
1 tablespoon milk
$^1/_2$ teaspoon vanilla extract
1 tablespoon cornstarch
3 cups confectioners' sugar

Combine all the ingredients and mix only until blended.

MAKES
ENOUGH
TO FROST
A 9 X 13-
INCH SHEET
CAKE

VERY LOW-FAT

Prep :10
Cook :00
Stand :00
Total :10

FRUIT COCKTAIL CAKE

2 cups all-purpose flour
1$^1/_2$ cups granulated sugar
1 teaspoon baking soda
1 teaspoon salt
2 cups (1 large can) fruit cocktail, light, juice and all
$^1/_4$ cup egg substitute
2 egg whites
1 teaspoon vanilla extract
1 cup firmly packed brown sugar
1 cup chopped pecans (optional)
Vanilla Dessert Sauce (recipe follows)

SERVES 12

0 GRAMS FAT
(WITHOUT
NUTS)

Prep :15
Cook :45
Stand :00
Total 1:00

Heat the oven to 325 degrees. Spray a 9 x 13 x 2-inch baking dish with vegetable oil cooking spray.

In a large bowl, combine the flour, sugar, baking soda, and salt. Mix with a whisk until thoroughly blended. Stir in the fruit cocktail (juice and all) and the egg substitute; set aside.

Beat the egg whites and vanilla until stiff. Fold into the fruit cocktail mixture until just combined. Pour into the prepared baking dish and sprinkle brown sugar and pecans over the batter. Bake for about 45 minutes, or until the center is springy to the touch. Cut into squares while still hot and serve with Vanilla Dessert Sauce.

VANILLA DESSERT SAUCE

Yum yum!!

**MAKES
ABOUT
1 CUP**

VERY LOW-FAT

**Prep :05
Cook :10
Stand :00
Total :15**

$^1/_2$ cup sugar
$^1/_2$ teaspoon vanilla extract
$^1/_2$ cup evaporated skim milk
$^1/_4$ cup Butter Buds (liquid form)

Combine all the ingredients in a medium saucepan and boil to the pudding stage, about 10 minutes. Pour over hot cake.

HERSHEY CAKE

1¼ cups all-purpose flour
⅓ cup unsweetened cocoa powder
1 teaspoon baking soda
6 tablespoons light margarine
1 cup sugar
1 cup skim milk
1 tablespoon white vinegar
½ teaspoon vanilla extract
Mocha Frosting (recipe follows)

SERVES 12

4 GRAMS FAT
WITH
FROSTING; 3
GRAMS
WITHOUT
FROSTING

Prep :15
Cook :35
Stand :00
Total :50

Preheat the oven to 350 degrees. Spray 2 round 8-inch cake pans or a 9 x 13-inch jelly roll pan with vegetable oil cooking spray.

In a bowl, mix the flour, cocoa, and baking soda. In a large saucepan, melt the margarine and stir in the sugar. Remove from the heat, add the milk, vinegar, and vanilla, and stir.

Add the dry ingredients to the saucepan and whisk until well blended. Pour evenly into the prepared pans. Bake until a toothpick inserted near the center comes out clean (two 8-inch pans for 20 minutes; the jelly roll pan about 30 to 35 minutes). Cool and frost.

MOCHA FROSTING

2^1/$_2$ cups confectioners' sugar, or more as needed
^{1}/$_4$ cup skim milk
2 tablespoons unsweetened cocoa powder
^{1}/$_2$ teaspoon vanilla extract
^{1}/$_4$ cup cold coffee

Mix above until smooth. Add more sugar if needed to reach spreading consistency.

HONEY CAKE

1 cup honey
1 cup applesauce
1 cup egg substitute
1^1/$_4$ cups sugar, divided
2^1/$_2$ cups all-purpose flour
1^1/$_2$ teaspoons baking powder
^{1}/$_2$ teaspoon baking soda
^{1}/$_2$ teaspoon instant coffee granules
^{1}/$_2$ cup hot water
^{1}/$_2$ teaspoon lemon extract
^{1}/$_2$ teaspoon almond extract
^{1}/$_4$ cup chopped pecans (optional)
^{1}/$_2$ teaspoon ground cinnamon

Preheat the oven to 350 degrees. Spray two 9-inch loaf pans with vegetable oil cooking spray and dust with flour. Set aside.

In a large mixing bowl, combine the honey, applesauce, egg substitute, and 1 cup of the sugar. Beat well.

In another bowl, whisk together the flour, baking powder, and baking soda. Gradually add to the honey mixture. Mix well. Dissolve the coffee granules in hot water and add to the batter. Stir in the lemon and almond extracts. Pour into the prepared loaf pans.

Combine the remaining $1/4$ cup of sugar with the pecans and cinnamon. Sprinkle over the loaves. Bake for 1 to $1^1/4$ hours, or until a toothpick inserted near the center of a loaf comes out clean. Cool in the pans 10 minutes before removing. Cool completely on wire racks.

HOT FUDGE SUNDAE PUDDING CAKE

"yum."

1 cup all-purpose flour
2 teaspoons baking powder
$1/4$ teaspoon salt
$3/4$ cup granulated sugar
$1/4$ cup plus $1^1/2$ tablespoons unsweetened cocoa powder, divided
$1/2$ cup skim milk
2 tablespoons Butter Buds, liquid form
1 teaspoon vanilla extract
1 cup pecans, chopped (optional)
$3/4$ cup firmly packed brown sugar
$1^3/4$ cups hot water

SERVES 4

3 GRAMS FAT

Prep :15
Cook :45
Stand :00
Total 1:00

Heat the oven to 350 degrees. Spray a 9-inch square baking pan with vegetable oil cooking spray.

In a large bowl, combine the flour, baking powder, salt, sugar, and $1^1/2$ tablespoons of the cocoa powder; mix well. Add the milk, Butter Buds, and vanilla; stir until blended. Stir in pecans if desired. Spread the mixture in the baking pan. Sprinkle the batter with brown sugar and the remaining ¼ cup cocoa mixed together. Pour hot water over. *Do not stir.*

Bake for 40 to 45 minutes. To serve, cut into squares while still hot and invert onto a serving dish. Top with fat-free ice cream or frozen yogurt. Spoon sauce remaining in the pan over the ice cream.

INDIVIDUAL HOT FUDGE SUNDAE CAKES

SERVES 6

1 GRAM FAT
EACH

Prep :15
Cook :25
Stand :00
Total :40

1 cup all-purpose flour
½ cup sugar
¼ cup plus 2 tablespoons unsweetened cocoa powder, divided
1½ teaspoons baking powder
⅔ cup skim milk
2 tablespoons fat-free margarine, melted
1 teaspoon vanilla extract
¾ cup firmly packed brown sugar
1½ cups hot water

Preheat the oven to 350 degrees.

Combine in a small bowl the flour, sugar, 2 tablespoons of cocoa, and the baking powder. Stir in the milk, margarine, and vanilla; mix until well blended. Spoon evenly into six 10-ounce custard cups. Place the cups in a 15 x 10 x 1-inch baking pan. Do not add water around, as is normal for baking custard dishes; this is just to make it easier to put in the oven, etc.

Combine the brown sugar and remaining ¼ cup of cocoa. Spoon 2 to 3 tablespoons of the mixture over the batter in each cup. Pour ¼ cup of hot water evenly over the sugar mixture in each cup. Do not stir!

Bake for 20 to 25 minutes, or until the centers of the cakes are set and firm to the touch. If desired, sprinkle with powdered sugar or top with fat-free ice cream or yogurt or light whipped topping.

LAZY DAZE OATMEAL CAKE

1³/₄ cups boiling water
1 cup rolled oats
¹/₂ cup Butter Buds, liquid form
1 cup granulated sugar
1 cup firmly packed brown sugar
1 teaspoon vanilla extract
¹/₂ cup egg substitute
1¹/₂ cups all-purpose flour
1 teaspoon salt
1 teaspoon baking soda
³/₄ teaspoon ground cinnamon

SERVES 8

4 GRAMS FAT

Prep :10
Cook :55
Stand :20
Total 1:25

Preheat the oven to 350 degrees. Spray a 9 x 13 x 2-inch baking dish with vegetable oil cooking spray and dust with flour.

Pour the boiling water over the oats. Let stand 20 minutes. Mix the Butter Buds with the sugars. Beat until fluffy. Blend in the vanilla and egg substitute. Stir in the oats.

Sift together the flour, salt, soda, and cinnamon. Add to the creamed mixture; mix well. Pour into the prepared baking dish. Bake for 50 to 55 minutes. Do not remove from the baking dish until serving.

LEMONLICIOUS CAKE

SERVES 12

5 GRAMS FAT
PER SERVING

Prep :10
Cook :35
Stand 3:00
Total 3:45

1 box light yellow cake mix
2 cups boiling water
1 (6-ounce) package sugar-free lemon-flavored gelatin dessert
Fluffy Lemon Pudding Frosting (recipe follows)

Prepare cake mix by the no-cholesterol directions on the package and bake as directed in 2 round pans. Take out of the pans and cool. Put the cakes back into the pans. Poke holes into the cakes with a fork.

Stir the boiling water into the gelatin mix in a medium bowl until dissolved. Pour half over each cake layer. Refrigerate at least 3 hours. Meantime, make the frosting.

When ready to frost, dip one cake pan in hot water for 10 seconds. Unmold onto a cake plate. Spread with about 1 cup of the frosting, Place the second layer on top of the first; frost top and sides of entire cake.

FLUFFY LEMON PUDDING FROSTING

MAKES
FROSTING
AND FILLING
FOR AN
8-INCH
2-LAYER
CAKE

VERY LOW-FAT

Prep :05
Cook :00
Stand :00
Total :05

1 cup cold skim milk
1 (4-serving) package instant lemon pudding mix
¹/₄ cup confectioners' sugar
1 (8-ounce) tub Lite Cool Whip topping

Pour the skim milk into a bowl. Add the lemon pudding mix and the confectioners' sugar. Beat with a wire whisk to blend. Stir in the Cool Whip topping until thoroughly combined.

PINEAPPLE-LEMON UPSIDE-DOWN CAKE

This is a cake you would want to cut in half, and as my friend says, "Don't stint yourself, just you take half and give me half." Light frozen (thawed) whipped topping may be served on top of this cake but will add a few fat grams.

SERVES 4

0 GRAMS FAT

Prep :15
Cook :30
Stand :00
Total :45

1 large can crushed pineapple, drained and juice reserved
1 (3-ounce) package sugar-free lemon-flavored gelatin
$^1/_2$ cup egg substitute
1 egg white
$^3/_4$ cup sugar
1 teaspoon vanilla extract
$^3/_4$ cup all-purpose flour
1 teaspoon baking powder
$^1/_4$ teaspoon salt

Heat the oven to 375 degrees. Line a round cake pan with waxed paper; spray with vegetable oil cooking spray. Spread the drained pineapple evenly in the pan. Sprinkle with the dry gelatin.

Beat the egg substitute and egg white in a medium bowl on high speed until very thick and lemon colored. Change to low speed and gradually add the sugar, $^1/_3$ cup of the reserved pineapple juice, and the vanilla. Slowly add the flour mixed with the baking powder and salt, beating on low speed just until the batter is smooth. Pour into the cake pan.

Bake 25 to 30 minutes, or until a toothpick inserted near the center comes out clean. Immediately loosen the side of the cake and invert it onto a plate. Remove the paper.

PINEAPPLE-ZUCCHINI CAKE

SERVES 10

1 GRAM FAT
(IF NUTS
OMITTED)

Prep :15
Cook :55
Stand :40
Total 1:40

2 cups shredded zucchini
1 cup (8-ounce can) crushed pineapple in juice
2 cups all-purpose flour
1¹/₂ cups sugar
2 teaspoons baking soda
2 teaspoons ground cinnamon
¹/₂ teaspoon salt
³/₄ teaspoon ground allspice
³/₄ cup egg substitute
³/₄ cup applesauce
¹/₃ cup thawed frozen pineapple juice concentrate
1 teaspoon vanilla extract
³/₄ cup chopped walnuts (optional)
¹/₂ cup golden raisins (optional)
Cream Cheese Frosting II (recipe follows)

Place the zucchini in a sieve; let it drain 30 minutes. Drain about half the syrup off the pineapple.

Preheat the oven to 350 degrees. Coat the inside of a 10-inch tube pan with vegetable oil cooking spray.

Stir together the flour, sugar, baking soda, cinnamon, salt, and allspice in a large bowl. Mix together the egg substitute, applesauce, pineapple juice concentrate, and vanilla in a small bowl. Add to the dry ingredients. Press the zucchini to remove excess liquid. Add drained zucchini and pineapple, walnuts, and raisins to the bowl. Mix with a wooden spoon until well blended. Turn into the prepared pan.

Bake for 50 to 55 minutes, or until a wooden pick inserted near the center comes out clean. Cool the cake in the pan on a wire rack for 10 minutes. Remove from the pan and cool on the rack completely.

Frost the cake with Cream Cheese Frosting II.

CREAM CHEESE FROSTING II

4 ounces fat-free cream cheese, at room temperature
2 cups confectioners' sugar
1¹/₂ teaspoons thawed frozen pineapple juice concentrate

   Combine all the ingredients in a small bowl. Stir carefully until spreading consistency.

MAKES
ENOUGH
TO FROST
A 10-INCH
TUBE CAKE

VERY LOW-FAT

Prep :05
Cook :00
Stand :00
Total :05

STRAWBERRY RHUBARB SHORTCAKE

This cake may be used as just a strawberry shortcake. Add berries and topping as desired. Yes!—Good!

Shortcake:
2¹/₄ cups reduced-fat baking and pancake mix, such as Bisquick
²/₃ cup skim milk
3 tablespoons Butter Buds, liquid form
3 tablespoons sugar, plus a little extra

Fruit:
¹/₂ pound fresh or frozen rhubarb, cut into ¹/₂-inch pieces
1 teaspoon cornstarch
¹/₂ cup sugar
1 pint strawberries, hulled and chopped, sweetened as desired (save 4 whole
    berries for garnish)
Cool Whip Lite Topping, thawed

SERVES 4

4 GRAMS FAT
PER SERVING

Prep :10
Cook :16
Stand :10
Total :36

About 1½ hours before serving or early in the day, make the shortcake:

Preheat the oven to 425 degrees. Spray an 8-inch round cake pan with vegetable oil cooking spray.

In a medium bowl with a fork, mix the baking mix, skim milk, Butter Buds, and 3 tablespoons of sugar until blended. Spoon the batter into the pan; sprinkle with extra sugar. Bake 15 minutes, or until the top is golden and a toothpick inserted in the center comes out clean. Cool the shortcake in the pan on a wire rack 10 minutes. Remove from the pan. Cool completely.

Meanwhile, prepare the fruit: In a 2-quart saucepan, over medium heat, cook the rhubarb, cornstarch, and ½ cup of sugar, stirring constantly until the mixture thickens and boils. Boil 1 minute, stir in strawberries, and remove from heat. Set aside to cool.

When the cake and strawberry mixture are both cool, they are ready to assemble. Cut the cake horizontally in half with a serrated knife. Place the bottom of the cake on a plate. Spoon the strawberry mixture over. Top with Cool Whip topping, spreading to the edge. Place the top of the cake on next.

Garnish with dollops of Cool Whip with a whole strawberry on each.

Pies

PIE CRUST

1$\frac{1}{2}$ cups all-purpose flour
$\frac{1}{2}$ teaspoon salt
$\frac{1}{3}$ cup canola oil
$\frac{1}{4}$ cup to $\frac{1}{2}$ cup cold skim milk

Mix the flour and salt in a shallow bowl. Beat the oil and $\frac{1}{4}$ cup milk together with a fork until creamy; pour over the flour and toss with a fork until blended. If the pastry is too dry to be gathered together, add more milk, 1 tablespoon at a time, until the pastry can be gathered into a ball.

Roll out on a floured board or between two sheets of waxed paper. Fit into pie plate and crimp edges. Fill with desired filling.

MAKES
ENOUGH
PASTRY
FOR A
SINGLE-
CRUST
8- OR 9-
INCH PIE

LOW-FAT

Prep :10
Cook :00
Stand :00
Total :10

LEAN PIE CRUST

MAKES
ENOUGH
PASTRY FOR
1 LARGE PIE
SHELL OR
COBBLER
CRUST

3 GRAMS FAT
PER SERVING

Prep :10
Cook :00
Stand 1:00
Total 1:10

1 cup all-purpose flour
$^1/_2$ teaspoon salt
$^1/_2$ teaspoon baking powder
$^1/_2$ cup (1 stick) light margarine, softened
$^1/_2$ cup plus 2 tablespoons cold skim milk

Stir together the flour, salt, and baking powder. Cut in the margarine with pastry blender. Add milk, and continue mixing until none sticks to the side of the bowl. Shape into a ball. Wrap in waxed paper and refrigerate 1 hour. Roll out on floured board and fit into pie plate. Trim and crimp edges.

GRAHAM CRACKER CRUST

SERVES 6

VERY LOW FAT

Prep :05
Cook :10
Stand :00
Total :15

$1^1/_4$ cups crushed fat-free graham crackers (20 crackers)
2 tablespoons sugar
1 tablespoon egg white ($^1/_2$ large white)
2 tablespoons canola oil
2 tablespoons unsalted butter, melted

Preheat the oven to 350 degrees.
Combine all the ingredients with 1 tablespoon of water and stir with a fork until evenly moistened.
Pour into a 9-inch pie shell and press with the fingers evenly on the bottom and up the sides.
Bake for 8 to 10 minutes, or until lightly browned. (The crust will firm up as it cools.)

MERINGUE PIE SHELL

2 egg whites, at room temperature
¹/₂ teaspoon vanilla extract
¹/₄ teaspoon cream of tartar
¹/₂ cup sugar

SERVES 6

0 GRAMS FAT

Prep :10
Cook 1:00
Stand 1:00
Total 2:10

Preheat the oven to 275 degrees.

In a small greasefree bowl, beat the egg whites until soft peaks form. Gradually add the vanilla, cream of tartar, and sugar. Beat at high speed until stiff and glossy. Spoon the meringue into a lightly sprayed 9-inch pie plate, building up around the sides (but not covering the rim) to form a pie shell.

Bake for 60 minutes. Turn off heat *Do not* open oven! Allow to dry in the oven for 60 minutes longer.

Cool the shell completely before filling. Fill with fresh fruit, fat-free pudding, or whatever you desire. Fat-free ice cream is also very good.

OVERNIGHT MERINGUE NESTS

6 egg whites
¹/₂ teaspoon cream of tartar
1¹/₄ cups sugar
¹/₄ cup chopped walnuts (optional)

SERVES 12

0 GRAMS FAT
WITHOUT
NUTS (2
GRAMS FAT
WITH NUTS)

Prep :10
Cook :00
Stand 8:00
Total 8:10

Heat the oven to 400 degrees. Line 2 cookie sheets with parchment or brown paper.

In a large bowl at high speed, beat the egg whites and cream of tartar until soft peaks form.

Gradually beat in the sugar, 1 tablespoon at a time, beating constantly until stiff and glossy.

Spoon the meringue into 12 mounds on the paper-lined cookie sheets, 4 inches apart. With the back of a spoon, shape into nests. Sprinkle with nuts if desired.

Place in the oven. *Turn the oven off. Do not open the oven door.* Let stand in the oven 8 hours or overnight.

To serve, place cooled nests on individual plates and fill with fat-free ice cream topped with favorite sauce.

BUTTERMILK PIE

SERVES 6

0.66 GRAM FAT (FILLING WITHOUT CRUST)

Prep :15
Cook :45
Stand :00
Total 1:00

2 cups sugar
2 tablespoons flour
1¼ cups egg substitute, lightly beaten
⅔ cup low-fat buttermilk (1 gram fat per cup)
½ cup Butter Buds, liquid form
1 teaspoon vanilla extract
1 unbaked pie shell (page 177)

Preheat the oven to 350 degrees.

Combine the sugar and flour in a bowl, add the egg substitute and buttermilk, and stir until blended. Stir in the Butter Buds and vanilla.

Pour into the prepared pie shell and bake for 45 minutes, or until the filling is set. Cool on a wire rack.

Tip: When mixing fat-free cream cheese, do so with a wire whisk carefully because it will break down to liquid if whipped too hard.

PINEAPPLE LAYER PIE

Crust:
1 cup all-purpose flour
1¹/₄ cups confectioners' sugar
¹/₄ cup almonds, finely chopped
¹/₃ cup (5 tablespoons plus 1 teaspoon) fat-free margarine

Filling:
1 (20-ounce) can crushed pineapple in juice
2 (8-ounce) packages Healthy Choice fat-free cream cheese, at room temperature
¹/₂ cup sugar
¹/₂ cup egg substitute

Topping:
¹/₄ cup all-purpose flour
¹/₄ cup sugar
¹/₂ cup light whipped topping

SERVES 12

VERY LOW-FAT

Prep :15
Cook :20
Stand 6:00
Total 6:35

Combine the crust ingredients. Pat into the bottom of a 12 x 8 x 2-inch baking dish. Bake at 350 degrees for 20 minutes.

Meanwhile, make the filling: Drain the pineapple and reserve the juice. In a bowl, mix the cream cheese until smooth. Stir in sugar, egg substitute, and ²/₃ cup of the reserved pineapple juice. Pour the filling over the hot crust. Bake at 350 degrees for 20 minutes. Cool.

Topping: Mix the flour and sugar in a saucepan; stir in 1 cup of reserved pineapple juice. Bring to a boil, stirring constantly with a wire whisk. Boil and stir for about 1 minute. Remove from the heat, fold in the pineapple, and cool. Fold in the whipped topping. Spread carefully over the cooled dessert. Refrigerate overnight or at least 5 to 6 hours.

LEAN PUMPKIN PIE

SERVES 6

0 GRAMS FAT
(FILLING
WITHOUT
CRUST)

Prep :15
Cook :55
Stand :00
Total 1:10

1³/₄ cups pumpkin or winter squash, cooked and mashed, well drained
1³/₄ cups evaporated skim milk
1 cup egg substitute
²/₃ cup firmly packed brown sugar
2 tablespoons granulated sugar
1 teaspoon salt
1¹/₄ teaspoons ground cinnamon
¹/₂ teaspoon ground ginger
¹/₂ teaspoon grated nutmeg
¹/₄ teaspoon ground cloves
Unbaked 9-inch pie shell (page 177)

Preheat the oven to 425 degrees.

Mix the pumpkin, skim milk, egg substitute, sugars, salt, and spices. Pour into the unbaked pie shell. Bake 10 minutes at 425 degrees, then lower the heat to 350 degrees and bake until a knife inserted in the center comes out clean, about 30 to 35 minutes longer. Cool on a rack.

TOFU PUMPKIN PIE

2 (10-ounce) packages firm tofu
²/₃ cup honey
2 egg whites (optional, for firmer pie)
1³/₄ cups canned pumpkin
2 teaspoons ground cinnamon
1 teaspoon grated nutmeg
¹/₂ teaspoon ground allspice
¹/₂ teaspoon ground ginger
¹/₄ teaspoon salt (scant) (optional)
9-inch unbaked pie shell (page 177)
Mock Whipped Cream (page 214)

SERVES 6

FILLING HAS 2
GRAMS FAT
(NO
CHOLESTEROL)

Prep :08
Cook 1:00
Stand :00
Total 1:08

Preheat the oven to 400 degrees.

Blend the tofu in a food processor or blender until creamy smooth. Add the honey, egg whites, pumpkin, spices, and salt; blend well. Pour into the unbaked pie shell. Bake about 1 hour, or until a toothpick inserted near the center comes out almost clean. Cool and serve with Mock Whipped Cream.

Cookies

LOW-FAT BROWNIES

SERVES 6

1 GRAM FAT
EACH

Prep :10
Cook :30
Stand :00
Total :40

1 cup egg substitute
$^1/_2$ cup canola oil
1 cup all-purpose flour
$^1/_3$ cup rolled oats
$^1/_2$ cup unsweetened cocoa powder
1 cup sugar
1 ripe banana, mashed
1$^1/_2$ teaspoons vanilla extract
$^1/_3$ cup chocolate chips

Preheat the oven to 350 degrees. Line a 9-inch square pan with aluminum foil.

Mix the egg substitute and the oil in a bowl. Beat in the flour, rolled oats, cocoa, sugar, banana, and vanilla. Fold in the chocolate chips. Pour into the prepared pan and bake for 25 to 30 minutes, until the brownies just begin to pull from the sides of the pan. Cool and cut into squares.

CARROT-DATE COOKIES

1½ cups chopped pitted dates
1 cup grated carrots
½ cup plain nonfat yogurt
¼ cup firmly packed brown sugar
1 tablespoon canola oil
1 teaspoon vanilla extract
1½ cups all-purpose flour
¼ cup Grape Nuts cereal
½ teaspoon baking soda
½ teaspoon salt

**MAKES
3 DOZEN**

1 GRAM FAT
PER COOKIE

Prep :10
Cook :15
Stand :15
Total :40

Preheat the oven to 350 degrees. Spray two baking sheets with vegetable oil cooking spray.

In a medium bowl stir together the dates, carrots, yogurt, sugar, oil, and vanilla. Let stand 15 minutes.

In another medium bowl mix the flour, Grape Nuts, baking soda, and salt. Using a wooden spoon, stir the dry ingredients into the date mixture until well blended. Drop by teaspoons 1½ inches apart onto the baking sheets. Bake about 15 minutes, or until the tops spring back when touched lightly. Cool on a wire rack.

CHEWY CRANBERRY COOKIES

The leavening reacts with the cranberries, so don't be surprised by the color of the cookies—they are still delicious!

**MAKES
4 DOZEN**

**0 GRAMS FAT
IF NUTS
OMITTED**

Prep :15
Cook :14
Stand :00
Total :29

1 cup sugar
¹/₄ cup fat-free margarine, softened
¹/₄ cup frozen apple juice concentrate, thawed and undiluted
2 egg whites
1¹/₂ teaspoons vanilla extract
1¹/₂ cups all-purpose flour
1 cup quick-cooking rolled oats, uncooked
1 teaspoon baking powder
1 teaspoon baking soda
¹/₂ teaspoon ground cinnamon
2 cups cranberries, coarsely chopped
¹/₂ cup walnuts, chopped (optional)

Preheat the oven to 350 degrees. Spray baking sheets lightly with vegetable oil cooking spray.

Cream the sugar and margarine, beating at medium speed until well blended. Add the apple juice concentrate, egg whites, and vanilla; beat well. Combine the flour, oats, baking powder, baking soda, and cinnamon. Gradually add to the creamed mixture, beating at low speed to form a soft dough. Stir in the cranberries and walnuts. Drop the dough by level tablespoonfuls 1 inch apart onto the baking sheets. Bake for 14 minutes, or until lightly browned. Remove from pans and cool on a rack.

CRANBERRY-PINEAPPLE BARS

1 cup cranberries
$^1/_4$ cup plus 3 tablespoons firmly packed brown sugar
1$^1/_2$ teaspoons cornstarch
1 (8-ounce) can crushed pineapple, undrained
$^3/_4$ cup all-purpose flour
$^3/_4$ cup quick-cooking oats, uncooked
$^1/_4$ teaspoon ground ginger
$^1/_4$ teaspoon ground cinnamon
3 tablespoons margarine, cut into small pieces and chilled
1 egg white, slightly beaten
3 tablespoons chopped pecans

SERVES 16

3 GRAMS FAT
PER SERVING

Prep :15
Cook :50
Stand :00
Total 1:05

Preheat the oven to 350 degrees. Spray an 8-inch square baking pan with vegetable oil cooking spray.

Mix the cranberries, 3 tablespoons of the brown sugar, the cornstarch, and the pineapple in a saucepan; stir well. Bring to a boil over medium heat; cook 1 minute. Cover, reduce the heat, and simmer 12 minutes, or until the cranberry skins pop and the mixture thickens, stirring occasionally. Set aside.

Combine the flour, the oats, $^1/_4$ cup of brown sugar, and the ginger and cinnamon in a bowl. Cut in the chilled margarine with a pastry blender until the mixture resembles coarse meal.

Reserve $^1/_2$ cup of the oat mixture. Combine the remaining oat mixture and egg white; stir well. Press the oat mixture into the bottom of the prepared baking pan. Bake for 10 minutes.

Spread the cranberry mixture over the hot crust. Combine the reserved oat mixture and pecans; sprinkle over the cranberry mixture. Bake for 27 minutes, or until lightly browned. Cool completely in the pan on a wire rack before cutting into squares.

Tips for Successful Meringues:
1. Beaters and bowls *must* be free and clean of any grease.
2. Separate egg whites carefully so as not to get any yellow parts.
3. Add sugar gradually.
4. Bake on paper-lined cookie sheets (either baking parchment or brown paper).
5. Wrap the meringues carefully in foil or place in a tightly covered container to store.
6. Fill *just* before serving.
7. Humid weather will adversely affect meringue performance. Hold off until a dry day if you can.

CHOCOLATE MERINGUES

**MAKES
ABOUT
30 SMALL
COOKIES**

0.10 GRAM
FAT EACH
COOKIE

Prep :15
Cook :45
Stand :00
Total 1:00

3 egg whites, at room temperature
$1/4$ teaspoon cream of tartar
6 tablespoons sugar, divided
$1/4$ cup unsweetened cocoa powder
2 teaspoons almond extract
1 cup crumbled shredded wheat biscuits

Preheat the oven to 275 degrees. Line two cookie sheets with parchment paper or brown paper.

Combine the egg whites with the cream of tartar in a medium bowl. Beat at high speed until soft peaks form. Gradually add 3 tablespoons of the sugar and continue to beat until stiff peaks form.

Mix the remaining 3 tablespoons of sugar and the cocoa. Gently fold into the egg whites. Fold in the almond extract and shredded wheat.

Drop by teaspoons about 2 inches apart onto the cookie sheets. Bake for 45 minutes, or until dry and set. Lift the meringues on the pan lining to a rack and allow to cool. Peel from the paper, using a spatula if needed.

DEVIL'S FOOD COOKIES

Prunes are not noticeable here; they help to carry a deep chocolate flavor.

MAKES 36

1 GRAM FAT
EACH

Prep :15
Cook :14
Stand :15
Total :44

$^1/_2$ cup pitted prunes
$^1/_2$ cup hot water
1$^1/_2$ cups sugar
$^1/_2$ cup plain nonfat yogurt
$^1/_4$ cup canola oil
2 egg whites, slightly beaten
1$^1/_2$ cups all-purpose flour
1 cup unsweetened cocoa powder
$^1/_2$ teaspoon salt
$^1/_2$ teaspoon baking soda
$^1/_2$ teaspoon instant coffee granules

Heat the oven to 350 degrees. Spray two baking sheets with vegetable oil cooking spray.

In a small bowl, soak prunes in the hot water for 10 to 15 minutes, until plump and soft. Place prunes and the soaking liquid in a blender; process until smooth.

In a medium bowl, whisk together the prune purée, sugar, yogurt, oil, and egg whites. In another bowl, mix the flour, cocoa, salt, soda, and coffee. Using a wooden spoon, mix the dry ingredients into the wet mixture just until blended.

Drop by tablespoons onto the prepared baking sheets 1$^1/_2$ inches apart. Bake for 12 to 14 minutes, or until the tops spring back when lightly touched. Cool on wire racks.

LAYERED FRUIT BARS

MAKES
9 BARS

3 GRAMS FAT
EACH

Prep :15
Cook :25
Stand :30
Total 1:10

Base and Topping:
$^1/_3$ cup solid vegetable shortening
$^1/_2$ cup firmly packed brown sugar
$^1/_4$ teaspoon vanilla extract
1 cup all-purpose flour
$^1/_8$ teaspoon salt (optional)
2 tablespoons skim milk
$^1/_4$ cup quick-cooking rolled oats (not instant or old-fashioned), uncooked

Filling:
1 cup apricot preserves

Glaze:
$^3/_4$ cup confectioners' sugar
$1^1/_2$ tablespoons skim milk
$^1/_4$ teaspoon vanilla extract

Heat the oven to 375 degrees.

For base: Cream the shortening, brown sugar, and vanilla in a large bowl. Mix in the flour, salt (if used), and milk. Reserve $^1/_4$ cup of the mixture for topping. Press the remaining mixture evenly in the bottom of an ungreased 8-inch square pan. Bake for 10 minutes, or until lightly browned.

For topping: Combine reserved $^1/_4$ cup of the base mixture with the oats until crumbly.

For filling: Spread the preserves over the hot baked base; sprinkle with topping. Bake for 15 minutes, or until the top is lightly browned. Cool completely.

For glaze: Combine powdered sugar, milk, and vanilla. Drizzle over top. Allow to set before cutting into bars.

LEMON SQUARES

Crust:
1 cup all-purpose flour
¹/₄ cup confectioners' sugar
4 tablespoons (¹/₄ cup) fat-free cream cheese, at room temperature
3 tablespoons canola oil

Filling:
3 large egg whites
³/₄ cup granulated sugar
1¹/₂ tablespoons grated lemon zest
2 tablespoons flour
¹/₂ teaspoon baking powder
¹/₂ teaspoon salt
¹/₃ cup fresh lemon juice

Confectioners' sugar for dusting over top

MAKES
9 BARS

3 GRAMS FAT
EACH

Prep :15
Cook :45
Stand :00
Total 1:00

Heat the oven to 350 degrees. Spray an 8-inch square baking pan with vegetable oil cooking spray.

Make the crust: Stir together the flour and sugar. Using a pastry blender or your fingertips, cut the cream cheese into the flour mixture until crumbly. Gradually add the oil, stirring with a fork until evenly moistened. (This mixture will be crumbly.) Press into the bottom of the prepared pan and bake for 20 to 25 minutes, or until light golden.

Meantime make the filling: Beat the egg whites, sugar, and lemon zest together until smooth. In a separate bowl, mix the flour, baking powder, and salt. Add to the egg white mixture and beat until smooth. Beat in the lemon juice. Pour over the hot crust and bake for about 20 minutes longer, or until the top is light golden and set.

Let cool in the pan. Spray a sharp knife with cooking spray and cut into squares. Dust with confectioners' sugar.

PEANUT BUTTER COOKIES

MAKES 36

3 GRAMS FAT
EACH

Prep :15
Cook :09
Stand :00
Total :24

²/₃ cup firmly packed brown sugar
¹/₂ cup smooth or chunky peanut butter
¹/₃ cup (5 tablespoons plus 1 teaspoon) light margarine, softened
¹/₄ cup egg substitute
¹/₂ cup cream of wheat cereal, uncooked (regular, instant, or quick)
1 teaspoon vanilla extract
1¹/₄ cups all-purpose flour
¹/₂ teaspoon baking soda

Preheat the oven to 350 degrees. Spray two baking sheets with vegetable oil cooking spray.

In a medium bowl, beat the brown sugar, peanut butter, margarine, and egg substitute until fluffy. Blend in the cereal and vanilla. Stir in the flour mixed with baking soda to make a stiff dough.

Drop by rounded spoonfuls on the prepared baking sheets, spacing the cookies about 2 inches apart. Flatten the balls with the bottom of a floured glass or fork. Bake for 8 to 9 minutes. Cool on wire racks.

PINEAPPLE COOKIES

MAKES 36

1 GRAM FAT
EACH

Prep :20
Cook :10
Stand :00
Total :30

2²/₃ cups all-purpose flour
1 teaspoon baking powder
¹/₂ teaspoon baking soda
¹/₃ cup (5 tablespoons plus 1 teaspoon) light margarine
¹/₂ cup sugar
¹/₄ cup egg substitute
1 teaspoon vanilla extract
¹/₄ teaspoon pineapple extract (optional)
¹/₄ cup low-fat pineapple yogurt

Preheat the oven to 425 degrees.

Sift the flour, baking powder, and baking soda; set aside. Cream the margarine and sugar until fluffy. Add the egg substitute, vanilla, and pineapple extract if using. Gradually add dry ingredients, alternating with the yogurt.

Form the dough into ball. Place on a floured surface. Roll out to ¼-inch thickness. Cut into desired shapes and place the cookies on two ungreased cookie sheets.

Bake for 8 to 10 minutes, or until lightly browned. Cool on a rack.

PUMPKIN COOKIES

³/₄ cup canned pumpkin purée
³/₄ cup firmly packed brown sugar
½ cup plain nonfat yogurt
2 tablespoons canola oil
1 teaspoon vanilla extract
1 cup raisins
2 cups sifted cake flour
1 teaspoon ground cinnamon
½ teaspoon ground ginger
½ teaspoon baking soda
½ teaspoon salt
¼ teaspoon ground allspice
¼ teaspoon grated nutmeg

MAKES 36

1 GRAM FAT
EACH

Prep :15
Cook :15
Stand :00
Total :30

Preheat the oven to 350 degrees. Spray two baking sheets with vegetable oil cooking spray.

Whisk together the pumpkin, sugar, yogurt, oil, and vanilla until smooth. Stir in the raisins.

In a separate bowl, mix the flour, cinnamon, ginger, soda, salt, allspice, and nutmeg. Using a wooden spoon, stir into the wet mixture until just blended.

Drop by tablespoons on baking sheets 1½ inches apart. Bake about 15 minutes, or until lightly browned. Cool on a wire rack.

S'MORES SQUARES

MAKES 15

2 GRAMS FAT
PER BAR

Prep :15
Cook :20
Stand :00
Total :35

Brownies:
24 graham crackers (12 whole crackers)
1 package low-fat fudge brownie mix
2 egg whites

Topping:
3 cups miniature marshmallows
$\frac{1}{2}$ cup milk chocolate chips
$\frac{1}{2}$ teaspoon shortening

Preheat the oven to 375 degrees. Spray a 15 x 10-inch jelly-roll pan with vegetable oil cooking spray. Line the bottom of the pan with graham crackers.

In a bowl combine the brownie mix, egg whites, and $\frac{1}{3}$ cup water, and stir until moistened, then beat 50 strokes by hand. Spread evenly over the graham crackers. Bake for 15 to 18 minutes. Do not overbake.

Remove brownies from the oven. Immediately sprinkle with marshmallows; gently press into hot brownies. Bake an additional 2 minutes, or until marshmallows are puffed.

Meanwhile, in a small saucepan, combine the chocolate chips and shortening. Stir over low heat until melted and smooth. Drizzle the topping over the marshmallows. Cool completely. Using a knife dipped in hot water, cut into bars.

ZUCCHINI COOKIES

$^1/_2$ cup (1 stick) light margarine
1 cup sugar
$^1/_4$ cup egg substitute
1 teaspoon vanilla extract
1$^1/_2$ cups all-purpose flour
$^1/_2$ teaspoon salt
$^1/_2$ teaspoon baking powder
$^1/_2$ teaspoon baking soda
$^1/_2$ teaspoon ground cinnamon
$^1/_4$ teaspoon ground cloves
$^1/_4$ teaspoon grated nutmeg
1$^1/_2$ cups rolled oats
1 cup grated zucchini, drained
1 cup nuts, chopped (optional)
$^1/_2$ cup raisins (optional)

MAKES 36

VERY LOW-FAT

Prep :15
Cook :12
Stand :00
Total :27

Preheat the oven to 350 degrees. Spray two cookie sheets with vegetable oil cooking spray.

In a large bowl, beat the margarine, sugar, egg substitute, and vanilla together until well blended. In a separate bowl, whisk the flour, salt, baking powder, baking soda, and spices together. Beat into the margarine-sugar mixture just enough to blend. Fold in the rolled oats, zucchini, and the nuts and raisins if using.

Drop by teaspoons onto the prepared cookie sheets. Bake for 10 to 12 minutes, or until lightly browned. Remove from pans and cool on a wire rack.

Desserts

CINNAMON APPLESAUCE

This will keep in the refrigerator for several weeks. A good do-ahead recipe.

1 large jar applesauce
1 medium package red hots

Mix the applesauce and red hots in a saucepan and stir over medium-low heat until the candy is melted. Cool before serving.

Variation: Serve over fat-free ice cream during the holidays for a quick festive dessert. Place a green maraschino cherry on top that has been cut in half, turned cut side up, and filled with brandy. Ignite the brandy for a grand finale.

SERVES 4

0 GRAMS FAT

Prep :02
Cook :12
Stand :00
Total :14

CINNAMON BREAD PUDDING

Stir the bread and milk gently if you like your bread pudding a little chunky. I like mine smoother so I smash mine.

5 cups cubed cinnamon bread, in 1-inch pieces
1/4 cup raisins
1 cup egg substitute
3/4 cup sugar
2 1/2 cups hot skim milk

Heat the oven to 375 degrees. Spray a 3-quart baking dish with vegetable oil cooking spray.

Combine the bread and raisins in the baking dish. Mix the egg substitute and sugar; add the hot milk. Pour over the bread and raisins and let stand about 5 minutes. Stir.

Bake for 25 to 35 minutes, or until the liquid is absorbed and pudding is set. Serve warm.

SERVES 8

2 GRAMS FAT
PER SERVING

Prep :10
Cook :35
Stand :05
Total :50

COLD BREAD PUDDING

SERVES 6

0 GRAMS FAT

Prep :10
Cook :60
Stand :00
Total 1:10

The reason this is called Cold Bread Pudding is that I also make it from leftover cold biscuits. Try it, but use the recipe in this book (page 148) for your biscuits.

8 slices fat-free bread
2 tablespoons flour
1$^1/_2$ cups sugar
1 cup egg substitute
1 tablespoon vanilla extract
4 cups skim milk
Raisins (optional)
Lemon Sauce (page 210) or Mocha Sauce (page 211), (optional)

Preheat the oven to 350 degrees. Spray a medium casserole with vegetable oil cooking spray.

Crumble the bread in a bowl and moisten with warm water (just enough to soften—about $^1/_4$ cup).

Mix the flour with the sugar and add to the bread crumbs along with the egg substitute. Stir in the vanilla and milk. Add raisins if desired.

Bake uncovered until set in the middle, about 45 to 60 minutes.

Serve with hot Lemon Sauce or Mocha Sauce.

ANGEL FOOD TRIFLE

Start this early in the day so you have plenty of time for chilling.

SERVES 8

0 GRAMS FAT

Prep :15
Cook :10
Stand 3:00
Total 3:25

¹/₃ cup sugar
¹/₄ cup cornstarch
¹/₄ teaspoon salt
2 cups skim milk
¹/₄ cup egg substitute
¹/₄ cup lemon juice
1 teaspoon grated lemon rind
2 (8-ounce) cartons nonfat vanilla yogurt
1 angel food cake, torn into bite-size pieces
¹/₂ cup sherry or Marsala wine (optional)
2 cups strawberries, hulled and sliced (reserve 3 whole berries)
3 kiwifruits, peeled and sliced

Combine the sugar, cornstarch, and salt in a saucepan. Gradually add the milk, stirring well. Cook over medium heat until the mixture begins to thicken, stirring constantly. Remove from the heat and gradually add the egg substitute, stirring constantly with a wire whisk. Cook over medium-low heat 2 minutes, while continuing to stir. Remove from the heat; cool slightly. Stir in lemon juice and rind.

Chill. Fold yogurt into the custard and refrigerate until ready to assemble the trifle.

Place ¹/₃ of the cake in a trifle bowl or a 2-quart serving dish. Sprinkle with ¹/₃ of the sherry. Spoon ¹/₃ of the custard over the cake; arrange half the strawberries and kiwi slices around the lower edge of the bowl and over the custard. Repeat, ending with 3 strawberries for decoration. Chill 2 hours before serving.

APPLE CRISP

SERVES 4

Almost any fruit can be substituted for the apples—peaches, plums, etc. You can even use canned fruit, such as cherries.

0 GRAMS FAT
(WITHOUT
NUTS)

Prep :15
Cook :45
Stand :00
Total 1:00

3 apples, peeled, cored, and cubed
2 to 4 tablespoons granulated sugar
Dash of cinnamon or nutmeg
$^1/_4$ cup quick-cooking rolled oats
2 tablespoons firmly packed brown sugar
$^1/_4$ cup whole wheat flour (or your can use regular flour)
2 tablespoons Butter Buds liquid
$^1/_4$ cup coarsely chopped pecans (optional)

Preheat the oven to 350 degrees.

Put the apples in an ungreased pie pan. Sweeten with sugar and add a touch of cinnamon or nutmeg.

Combine the rolled oats, brown sugar, flour, Butter Buds, and chopped nuts. Sprinkle over the apples. Bake for 45 minutes, or until tender and golden brown. (Or you can microwave 4 to 6 minutes.)

BAKED RICE CUSTARD

²/₃ cup sugar
2 tablespoons cornstarch
¹/₄ teaspoon salt
2³/₄ cups skim milk
¹/₂ cup egg substitute
1 egg white
¹/₄ cup raisins
1 cup cooked white rice (leave out salt and butter)
¹/₂ teaspoon vanilla extract
¹/₈ teaspoon grated nutmeg

SERVES 6

1 GRAM FAT
PER ¹/₂ CUP
SERVING

Prep :25
Cook :55
Stand 3:00
Total 4:20

Heat the oven to 325 degrees. Coat a 1¹/₂-quart baking dish with vegetable oil cooking spray.

Combine sugar, cornstarch, and salt; set aside. Put the milk in a heavy saucepan; place over medium heat, stirring constantly until almost boiling. Remove from heat; gradually stir in the sugar mixture.

Beat egg mixture and egg white together until frothy. Gradually stir ¹/₄ of the hot mixture into the egg substitute; then add to remaining hot mixture, stirring constantly. Stir in raisins, rice, and vanilla. Pour into the prepared baking dish.

Place the baking dish in a large shallow pan. Add water to a depth of about 1 inch. Bake for 30 minutes. Stir gently and bake 10 more minutes. Stir gently again, sprinkle with nutmeg, and bake 10 to 15 minutes longer, or until a knife inserted near the center comes out clean. Remove the pudding dish from the water bath; cool.

Cover and chill 3 to 4 hours before serving.

CHERRIES JUBILEE

SERVES 6

0 GRAMS FAT

Prep :10
Cook :10
Stand :00
Total :20

1 (16-ounce) can pitted dark sweet cherries, undrained
1 tablespoon cornstarch
¼ cup brandy
Fat-free frozen yogurt or ice cream

Drain the cherries, reserving juice. In a skillet, combine the liquid from the cherries with the cornstarch. Blend well with a wire whisk. Add the cherries. Heat until the liquid boils and thickens, stirring occasionally. Transfer the cherry mixture to a heatproof serving dish.

Heat the brandy in a small saucepan; pour over the hot cherries and carefully ignite. Take flaming to the table.

Serve over frozen yogurt or ice cream.

CHOCOLATE PUDDING

SERVES 4

**1 GRAM FAT
PER SERVING**

Prep :05
Cook :12
Stand :00
Total :17

2 cups skim milk
2 tablespoons unsweetened cocoa powder
3 tablespoons sugar
¼ teaspoon salt
2½ tablespoons cornstarch
2 tablespoons vanilla extract
Overnight Meringue Nests (page 179) (optional)

Scald 1½ cups of the milk in medium saucepan. Combine the cocoa, sugar, salt, and cornstarch in a small bowl. Blend the remaining ½ cup of cold milk into the cocoa mixture. Mix well. Stir into scalded milk.

Cook over very low heat, stirring constantly, until the mixture is thick. Remove from the heat. Stir in vanilla. Spoon into individual dessert dishes or Overnight Meringue Nests.

FRUIT COBBLER

1 pound fruit (peaches, apples, cherries, or blueberries)
Sugar
Lemon juice
1 cup all-purpose flour
¹/₄ cup egg substitute
³/₄ cup Butter Buds liquid

SERVES 4

LESS THAN
1 GRAM FAT

Prep :10
Cook :40
Stand :00
Total :50

Heat the oven to 350 degrees. Spray a 9-inch square baking dish with vegetable oil cooking spray.

Peel and slice the fruit (you should have about 2¹/₂ cups). Add sugar to taste, plus a few drops of lemon juice to peaches, blueberries, or apples. Dump into the baking dish.

Topping or crust: Mix the flour, 1 cup of sugar, and the egg substitute with a fork until crumbly. Pour over the fruit.

Pour Butter Buds liquid over this (stringing it around evenly) and bake for about 35 to 40 minutes, until golden brown.

FRUIT COBBLER WITH CREAM CHEESE PASTRY DOUGH

1 cup sifted cake flour
1 teaspoon sugar, plus 1 tablespoon sugar for sprinkling on top
¹/₂ teaspoon salt
¹/₄ cup Healthy Choice fat-free cream cheese
4 teaspoons light margarine
2¹/₂ to 3 tablespoons skim milk, plus 1 tablespoon for glaze
2¹/₂ cups prepared fruit (peaches, apples, blueberries, and/or cherries, peeled, pitted, and sliced if necessary)

SERVES 6

1 GRAM FAT
PER SERVING

Prep :15
Cook :45
Stand :30
Total 1:30

Heat the oven to 350 degrees. Grease a 9-inch deep-dish pie plate with cooking spray.

Mix flour, 1 teaspoon sugar, and salt. With a pastry cutter, cut the cream cheese and margarine into the flour mixture until crumbly. With a fork, stir in enough milk until clumped together. Press the dough into a circle, wrap in plastic, and refrigerate for at least ½ hour. (Can be made ahead and stored up to 2 days.)

On a lightly floured surface, roll the pastry to ⅛-inch thickness. Put the fruit into the prepared pie plate. Carefully place the dough over the fruit and tuck in the edges. Brush the top with milk and sprinkle 1 tablespoon sugar over. Cut several slashes for steam vents.

Bake about 45 minutes or until the pastry is golden and filling is bubbly.

Cool slightly and serve with fat-free ice cream or frozen yogurt.

FRUIT DUMPLINGS

I scream, you scream, we all scream for more.

SERVES 4

VERY LOW-FAT

Prep :20
Cook :25
Stand :00
Total :45

Dough:
1 cup all-purpose flour
3 tablespoons sugar
1 teaspoon baking powder
½ teaspoon baking soda
⅛ teaspoon salt
½ cup low-fat buttermilk (1 gram fat per cup)
1 tablespoon Butter Buds, liquid form
1 tablespoon canola oil

Fruit Mixture:
2 pints any fruit
½ cup sugar
4 teaspoons lemon juice
½ teaspoon ground cinnamon mixed with 1 tablespoon sugar

To make the dough: Mix the flour, sugar, baking powder, soda, and salt. In a small bowl mix the buttermilk, Butter Buds, and oil.

Make a well in the center of the flour mixture and add the liquid mixture, mixing just until combined. Set aside.

Make the fruit mixture: In a heavy skillet combine the fruit, sugar, and lemon juice with ¼ cup water. Toss gently, cover, and bring to a boil. Reduce the heat to low; remove the cover. Drop dumpling batter by spoonfuls evenly over the simmering fruit. Sprinkle with cinnamon-sugar mixture. Cover the pan tightly with a lid or foil and cook for 15 to 17 minutes, or until dumplings are firm to the touch.

Serve hot with fat-free frozen yogurt or ice cream.

QUICK FRUIT DESSERT

1 (16-ounce) can fruit pie filling
1 tablespoon lemon juice
1 cup fat-free granola
⅓ cup all-purpose flour
2 tablespoons Butter Buds liquid

SERVES 2

0 GRAMS FAT

Prep :05
Cook :25
Stand :00
Total :30

Preheat the oven to 375 degrees.

Mix the pie filling and lemon juice and pour into an ungreased 8-inch square pan, spreading evenly.

Mix the granola, flour, and Butter Buds; sprinkle over the filling. Bake uncovered 20 to 25 minutes, or until the filling is bubbly and topping is golden brown.

Serve warm with fat-free ice cream or frozen yogurt.

STRAWBERRY DELIGHT

SERVES 12

1 GRAM FAT PER SERVING

Prep :20
Cook :20
Stand 4:30
Total 5:10

2 cups finely chopped fat-free pretzels
1/3 cup plus 1/4 cup sugar
2/3 cup fat-free margarine, melted
12 ounces Healthy Choice fat-free cream cheese
2 tablespoons skim milk
1 cup Lite Cool Whip, thawed
1 (8-ounce) package sugar-free strawberry-flavored gelatin
2 cups boiling water
1 1/2 cups cold water
2 pints strawberries, hulled and sliced
Chopped English walnuts, for garnish

Preheat the oven to 350 degrees.

Mix the crushed pretzels, 1/3 cup sugar, and the melted margarine. Press firmly into the bottom of a 9 x 13 x 2-inch baking pan. Bake for 15 to 20 minutes. Allow to cool.

Mix the cream cheese, the remaining 1/4 cup of sugar, and the milk until smooth. Stir in the Cool Whip. Spread over the cooled crust and refrigerate.

Mix the gelatin and boiling water in a bowl until dissolved; add the cold water. Refrigerate 1 to 1 1/2 hours, or until slightly thickened. Stir in the strawberries. Spoon over the cream cheese layer. Be careful not to let it get too thick.

Refrigerate for 3 hours, or until firm. Cut into squares and add a dollop of Lite Cool Whip and sprinkle a few chopped English walnuts over the Cool Whip.

SUNDAY DELIGHT

A good do-ahead recipe. Pretty for the holidays with the red cherries.

6 egg whites
³/₄ teaspoon cream of tartar
2 cups sugar
2 cups crushed fat-free soda crackers (about 45)
³/₄ cup nuts, chopped
2 teaspoons vanilla extract
2 cups Lite Cool Whip, thawed
1 (21-ounce) can cherry pie filling (see Note)

SERVES 12

4 GRAMS FAT
PER SERVING

Prep :20
Cook :25
Stand 4:20
Total 5:05

Heat the oven to 350 degrees. Spray a 9 x 13 x 2-inch baking dish thoroughly with vegetable oil cooking spray.

Beat the egg whites until frothy, add the cream of tartar, then gradually add sugar. Beat until stiff. Carefully fold in the crushed crackers, nuts, and vanilla.

Spread in the prepared dish and bake for 25 minutes. Cool on a wire rack.

Spread the Cool Whip over the cooled first layer, then spoon cherries over the Cool Whip, dotting and stringing around.

Chill several hours before serving.

Note: I use 2 cans of cherries. We like more cherries to completely cover the top of the dessert.

ORANGE-MELON SALAD

SERVES 2

0 GRAMS FAT

Prep :20
Cook :00
Stand :15
Total :35

2¹/₂ cups honeydew melon cubes or balls
3 oranges, peeled and cut up
¹/₃ cup (3 ounces) frozen limeade concentrate, thawed

In a serving bowl, combine all the ingredients. Cover; refrigerate until serving time.

WINE GELATIN

SERVES 8

0 GRAMS FAT

Prep :00
Cook :05
Stand 2:00
Total 2:05

2 packets unflavored gelatin
¹/₄ cup sugar
¹/₄ cup cold water
3 cups red wine
1 teaspoon grated lemon rind
Mock Whipped Cream (page 214)
2 to 3 tablespoons brandy

Mix the gelatin and sugar in a heavy saucepan. Gradually add the cold water. Stir over low heat until dissolved. Remove from the heat; add the wine and lemon zest.

Divide among 8 wineglasses and allow to set. Chill until firm. Top with Mock Whipped Cream flavored with the brandy.

FRUIT DIP

1 (8-ounce) package fat-free cream cheese, softened
³/₄ cup firmly packed brown sugar
¹/₄ cup granulated sugar
1 tablespoon vanilla extract
¹/₂ cup chopped nuts (optional)

Stir the cream cheese with the sugars and vanilla until creamy. Fold in the nuts if using. Serve with apple wedges or any kind of fruit desired.

MAKES
ABOUT
2 CUPS

0 GRAMS FAT,
WITHOUT
NUTS

Prep :05
Cook :00
Stand :00
Total :05

PINEAPPLE ALMOND FRUIT DIP

1 (8-ounce) carton fat-free cream cheese
³/₄ cup crushed and drained canned pineapple
1 tablespoon firmly packed brown sugar
1¹/₂ teaspoons almond extract

Blend all the above only until smooth. Serve with sliced apples or any fresh fruit; also good with celery and crackers (fat-free of course).

Note: Be careful blending fat-free cream cheese and sour cream—they will break down to liquid very easily.

SERVES 1

0 GRAMS FAT

Prep :05
Cook :00
Stand :00
Total :05

CHOCOLATE SAUCE

Excellent over nonfat frozen yogurt or ice cream.

MAKES 1
CUP
SAUCE

0.6 GRAM FAT

Prep :05
Cook :10
Stand :00
Total :15

¹/₂ cup unsweetened cocoa powder
¹/₂ cup firmly packed light brown sugar
³/₄ cup skim milk
1 teaspoon vanilla extract

In a saucepan, mix the cocoa powder and sugar. Blend in the milk. Over medium heat, heat to boiling, stirring constantly. Lower heat and simmer, stirring constantly, for about 5 minutes or just until thickened. Cool; stir in vanilla. Serve at room temperature.

LEMON SAUCE

SERVES 4

0 GRAMS FAT

Prep :05
Cook :05
Stand :00
Total :10

¹/₂ cup sugar
2 tablespoons cornstarch
¹/₄ cup lemon juice
¹/₂ teaspoon grated lemon rind

In a heavy saucepan, combine the sugar and cornstarch; stir well. Gradually whisk in lemon juice and 1¹/₄ cups water. Set over moderate heat and bring to boil. Reduce heat to low and cook, stirring constantly, until the sauce is thickened and clear (about 2 to 3 minutes).

Remove from heat, cool, and stir in lemon rind.

Lemon Raisin Sauce: Add 2 tablespoons raisins.

Orange Sauce: Use 1¹/₂ cups orange juice instead of the lemon juice and water. Use orange rind instead of lemon rind.

MOCHA SAUCE

Serve over frozen chocolate fat-free yogurt or ice cream, fruit, cake, or bread pudding.

SERVES 4

¹/₂ cup sugar
¹/₃ cup unsweetened cocoa powder
¹/₃ cup light corn syrup
2¹/₂ tablespoons semisweet chocolate morsels
1 teaspoon instant coffee granules
¹/₂ teaspoon vanilla extract

0.9 GRAM FAT
PER TEASPOON

Prep :05
Cook :10
Stand :00
Total :15

Combine the sugar, cocoa, and corn syrup with ¹/₃ cup of water in a saucepan. Bring to a boil over medium heat, stirring frequently. Add the chocolate morsels and coffee granules; stir until melted. Remove from heat and cool. Stir in vanilla.

WHISKEY SAUCE

1 cup sugar
¹/₄ cup whiskey
¹/₄ cup nonfat vanilla yogurt

SERVES 8

0 GRAMS FAT

Combine sugar with 1 cup of water; mix well. Bring to a boil and cook for 5 minutes. Remove from the heat and stir in whiskey. Cool to lukewarm. Stir in the yogurt. Serve warm over bread pudding or frozen ice cream or yogurt.

Prep :05
Cook :05
Stand :00
Total :10

Variation: Substitute ¹/₄ cup water and 1 teaspoon brandy extract for the whiskey. Yum.

HOMEMADE EGG SUBSTITUTE

This is good for an emergency, but I have found the commercial egg substitutes that are now on the market and are fat-free to be much faster and easier.

MAKES
³/₄ CUP

2.4 GRAMS FAT

Prep :10
Cook :00
Stand :00
Total :10

6 egg whites
¹/₄ cup instant nonfat dry milk powder
2 tablespoons water
1¹/₂ teaspoons vegetable oil
¹/₄ teaspoon ground turmeric

Combine all the ingredients in the container of electric blender. Process 30 seconds. Refrigerate up to 1 week or freeze in an airtight container for up to 1 month.

MOCK SOUR CREAM

1 cup nonfat cottage cheese
2 tablespoons fat-free mayonnaise
Juice and grated zest of ¹/₂ lemon
¹/₄ cup skim buttermilk

Blend all ingredients together until smooth.

SERVES 1

LOW-FAT

Prep :05
Cook :00
Stand :00
Total :05

MOCK WHIPPED CREAM

SERVES 2

0 GRAMS FAT

Prep :10
Cook :00
Stand 1:00
Total 1:10

1¹/₂ teaspoons unflavored gelatin
¹/₄ cup boiling water
1¹/₂ teaspoons honey
1 cup ice water
¹/₂ cup nonfat dry milk powder
2 teaspoons vanilla extract

Chill a large bowl and beaters. Dissolve the gelatin in boiling water. Stir in the honey. Cool and then chill until syrupy.

In the chilled bowl, beat together the ice water, nonfat dry milk powder, and vanilla until very frothy. Gradually add the cooled gelatin mixture and continue beating until quite stiff. Chill for at least 1 hour before using.

This will keep in the refrigerator for about a day.

HOT APPLE CIDER

SERVES 8

0 GRAMS FAT

Prep :05
Cook :40
Stand :00
Total :45

An old favorite for the holidays or entertaining; makes the house smell great.

2 quarts apple cider
¹/₄ cup firmly packed brown sugar
¹/₂ teaspoon grated nutmeg
2 cinnamon sticks
Peel of 1 orange

Combine all the ingredients in large pan. Bring to a boil. Reduce the heat and simmer for 30 to 40 minutes. Remove cinnamon sticks and orange peel. Keep warm in thermos pitcher or coffeepot.

APPLE BUTTER

This is worth making just to enjoy the spiced apple aroma while cooking, especially around the holidays. It's tart, because it has no sugar. You can add sweetener if desired.

0 GRAMS FAT

1 quart apple cider
8 large Granny Smith apples
12 whole allspice berries
1 whole cinnamon stick

Prep :15
Cook 2:15
Stand :00
Total 2:30

In a large heavy saucepan, boil the cider uncovered until reduced to 2 cups. Remove stems from apples but do *not* peel or core them. Cut into chunks and add to the cider. Add the allspice and cinnamon tied in a cheesecloth bag.

Bring to a boil, reduce heat to low, and simmer, uncovered, until soft, about 20 minutes. Press the apples through a strainer or food mill into a bowl. Return the pulp to the saucepan along with the spices. Simmer, stirring often, until the butter is very thick, about 1¾ hours. Discard the allspice and cinnamon. Let cool.

May be stored, covered, in refrigerator for up to 2 weeks.

EGGNOG

SERVES 12

1 GRAM FAT

Prep :10
Cook :15
Stand 2:00
Total 2:25

Eggs I know—but what's nog? Nog, says the Oxford Dictionary, is an English word of obscure origin meaning strong ale, dating to the seventeenth century.

1¹/₂ cups sugar
¹/₄ cup flour
Pinch of salt
4 large eggs
2 egg whites
8 cups skim milk, scalded
2 teaspoons vanilla extract
¹/₂ to 1 cup brandy, rum, or whiskey (optional)
Freshly grated nutmeg

Whisk the sugar, flour, and salt in a large heavy nonaluminum saucepan. Add the eggs and whites; whisk until smooth. Gradually whisk in the milk. Cook over low heat, stirring with a wooden spoon, for 15 minutes, or until thick enough to coat spoon. Remove immediately from the heat and strain into a bowl. Cover and refrigerate until chilled, at least 2 hours or overnight.

Before serving, stir in the vanilla and liquor. Pour 2 cups of custard into a blender. Add 2 ice cubes and blend until frothy. Repeat with remaining custard. Serve immediately, topped with a dusting of nutmeg.

LOW-FAT EGGNOG

4 cups skim milk
1 (12-ounce) can evaporated skim milk
1 (8-ounce) carton egg substitute
$^1/_2$ cup sugar
$^1/_3$ cup light rum
1 teaspoon vanilla extract
Grated nutmeg

SERVES 6

1 GRAM FAT
PER CUP

Prep :05
Cook :12
Stand 24:00
Total 24:17

   Over medium heat stir the skim milk, evaporated milk, egg substitute, and sugar for about 10 minutes, or until slightly thickened. *Do not boil.* Stir over bowl of ice for about 2 minutes. Cover. Chill for 4 to 24 hours.
   Stir in the rum and vanilla. Add more skim milk if needed for desired thickness. Sprinkle with nutmeg.

GARLIC WINE

Good on salad. Excellent to cook with.

6 to 8 whole cloves garlic, peeled
1 bottle red wine

SERVES 10

0 GRAMS FAT

Prep :00
Cook :00
Stand :00
Total :00

   Put garlic into wine; let stand for 3 to 4 weeks before using.

HINTS AND TIPS

If you have a slight drain problem, try pouring a cup of salt and a cup of baking soda along with a kettleful of boiling water down it. The grease will usually dissolve enough so that you can get by until you can get a plumber.

If you have rust spots on your stainless steel sink, try using lighter fluid to remove them. Then be sure you clean the lighter fluid off.

When you have half an onion left, drop it in a plastic bag and put in the freezer. I keep a bag for just all sorts of leftover veggies, then I just dump them into soup or stew, frozen. Carrots, potatoes, peas, any such veggies.

Keep popcorn in the freezer; it keeps it fresh longer and eliminates old maids.

When cooking rice, drop in a pinch of rosemary; it will add an interesting flavor.

If you need to take hot food to a church function, funeral dinner, or picnic, etc., wrap it in a double thickness of foil and put it in an ice chest. The Styrofoam chest will keep it hot for quite some time. When we have our large family get-togethers, we put hot boiled corn, shrimp, or whatever we are cooking for a crowd in a clean foam chest and set it right on the picnic table. Food stays hot as can be.

We sometimes spill wine on our nicest tablecloth. Don't let it spoil your day—try mounding ordinary table salt on the spill. When dry just brush away. The salt will absorb the wine.

Spray garbage sacks or trash cans with ammonia; will keep dogs from getting into them.

INDEX

Cucumbers, 45-46
  Creamy, 46
Cupcakes, Chocolate Creamy,
    163
Custard, Baked Rice, 201

Date:
  Carrot Cookies, 185
  Cherry Quick Bread, 152
Defatting, 18, 19
Desserts, 13, 155-211
  Angel Food Trifle, 199
  Apple Crisp, 200
  Baked Rice Custard, 201
  Cherries Jubilee, 202
  Cinnamon Applesauce, 197
  Fruit Cobbler, 203
  Fruit Cobbler with Cream Cheese
    Pastry Dough, 203
  Fruit Dip, 209
  Fruit Dumplings, 204
  Orange-Melon Salad, 208
  Pineapple Almond Fruit Dip,
    209
  Quick Fruit, 205
  Strawberry Delight, 206
  Sunday Delight, 207
  Wine Gelatin, 208
  see also Cakes; Cookies; Frostings;
    Pies (dessert); Puddings; Sauces
    (dessert)
Devil's Food Cookies, 189
Dijon Chicken, 62
Dill(ed):
  Garden Dip, 28
  Mushroom Chicken, 66
Dips:
  Baked Southern, 27
  Chunky Vegetable Salsa, 31
  Dilled Garden, 28
  Fiesta, 29
  for fruit, 209
  Guacamole, 29
  Layered Tex Mex, 30
  Onion Salsa, 32
  Salsa Verde, 32
  Thick and Creamy, 28
Dressings, 59
  Corn Bread, 60, 82
  see also Salad dressings
Dumplings:
  Chicken and, 70
  Fruit, 204

Egg(s), 19, 24, 100-104
  Breakfast Ham Casserole, 96
  Breakfast Sausage Bake, 92
  Breakfast Sausage Casserole, 92
  Italian Omelet, 103
  Overnight French Toast, 154
  Pocket Breakfast, 104
  Substitute, Homemade, 213
  see also Meringue(s); Quiche
Eggnog, 216
  Low-Fat, 217
Exercise, 21, 22

Fat, 21
  calculating percentage of calories
    from, 20
  counting grams of, 20
  hints for reducing intake of, 12–13,
    18-20, 22-24
Festive Corn Salad, 47
Fiesta Dip, 29
Fiesta Quiche, 101
Fish:
  Baked "Fried" Catfish, 98
  fat content of, 97
French Fries, Fake, 139
French Toast, Overnight, 154
"Fried":
  Catfish, Baked, 98
  Cornmeal-Coated Chicken, 64
Fried Corn Bread, 151
Frostings, 19
  Cream Cheese, 165, 175
  Fluffy Lemon Pudding, 172
  Mocha, 168
  Vanilla, 156, 162
Fruit, 21
  Bars, Layered, 190
  Cobbler, 203
  Cocktail Cake, 165
  Dessert, Quick, 205
  dips for, 209
  Dumplings, 204
  see also specific fruits

Garlic:
  Dressing, Creamy, 55
  Toast, 67
  Wine, 217
Gelatin, Wine, 208
German Potato Salad, 49
Glazes, 158, 190
  Lemon Honey, 59